PERFORMING
BAROQUE MUSIC

Attributed to Constantin Netscher (1688–1723), "Portrait de Johann Schenck, musicien de l'Electeur Palatin," oil on canvas, 69 cm × 52 cm, Conservation du château et des Musées de Blois, France. Johannes Schenck (1660–1712), a composer and virtuoso performer on the viola da gamba, worked at the court in Düsseldorf.

Performing Baroque Music

MARY CYR

Scolar Press

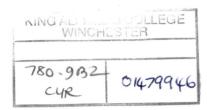
Front endpaper illustration
The tempest from the opera *Alcyone* (1706) by Marin Marais, with an indication for double bass in the orchestra, a novelty at the time. From the copy in the Music Library, University of California, Berkeley.

Back endpaper illustration
The instrumental parts for three viols and lute from the song "Cease leaden slumber" by Tobias Hume (*Poeticall Musicke,* London, 1607). The instrumental parts were printed in this manner to permit the players to read from a single book.

Jacket illustration
Johann Georg Platzer (1704–1761), "Das Konzert," oil on copper 58 × 84 cm, Nürnberg, Germanisches National Museum. Platzer's capricious concert by a singer and several instrumentalists exhibits several features of the rococo style, including assymetry, contrasts of various types, and the shell motive. The painting on the wall illustrates the mythical contest between Apollo and Marsyas.

Copyright © 1992 by Amadeus Press
(an imprint of Timber Press, Inc.)

Published by
SCOLAR PRESS
Gower House
Croft Road
Aldershot
Hants GU11 3HR
England

British Library CIP data is available

ISBN 0 85967 960 8

Contents

List of Musical Examples

List of Tables

List of Figures

Abbreviations

Middle C is shown as c^1; the C above middle C is c^2, and the Cs below middle C are c, C, and C^1.

ca.	circa
ch.	chapter
ed.	edition, editor, edited by
ex.	example
facs.	facsimile
fl.	flourished
fol.	folio
m.	measure
mm.	measures
no.	number
nos.	numbers
op.	opus
p.	page
pp.	pages
R	reprint
suppl.	supplement
trans.	translation, translator, translated by
v.	volume, volumes

PERIODICALS AND OTHER GENERAL BIBLIOGRAPHY

BGA   *J. S. Bach Werke.* Ed. Bach-Gesellschaft. 47 v. Leipzig: Breitkopf & Härtel, 1851–1899. R Farnsborough: Gregg International, 1968.

BJ   *Bach-Jahrbuch* (Leipzig, 1904–)

BWV   Schmieder, Wolfgang. *Thematisch-Systematisches Verzeichnis der musikalischen Werke Johann Sebastian Bach: Bach-Werke-Verzeichnis.* Wiesbaden: Breitkopf & Härtel, 1990.

CorelliW   Corelli, Arcangelo. *Historische-kritische Gesamtausgabe der musikalischen Werke* (1987–).

CMS   *College Music Symposium* (1961–)

DDT   *Denkmäler Deutscher Tonkunst.* 65 v. Ed. Max Seiffert (Leipzig: Breitkopf & Härtel, 1892–1931). R Wiesbaden: Breitkopf & Härtel, 1958– .

DTÖ   *Denkmäler der Tonkunst in Österreich.* 117 v. Ed. Guido Adler (Vienna: Artaria, 1894–). R Graz, Austria: Akademische Druck-u. Verlagsanstalt, 1959–).

EM   *Early Music* (London, 1973–)

Grove   *The New Grove Dictionary of Music and Musicians.* Ed. Stanley Sadie. 20 v. London: Macmillan, 1980.

GroveInstr   *The New Grove Dictionary of Musical Instruments.* Ed. Stanley Sadie. 3 v. London: Macmillan, 1984.

HandelW   *Hallische Händel-Ausgabe.* Kassel: Bärenreiter, 1955– .

JAMIS   *Journal of the American Musical Instrument Society* (1974–)

JAMS   *Journal of the American Musicological Society* (1948–)

JLSA   *Journal of the Lute Society of America* (1968–)

JRME   *Journal of Research in Music Education* (1953–)

MacClintock   MacClintock, Carol. *Readings in the History of Music in Performance.* Bloomington: Indiana University Press, 1979.

ML   *Music and Letters* (1920–)

MonteverdiW   Malipiero, G. Francesco. *Tutte le opere di ClaudioMonteverdi,* 16 v. Asolo: n.p., 1926–1942. R Vienna: Universal Edition, 1967.

MR   *The Music Review* (1940–)

NBA   *Neue Ausgabe sämtlicher Werke [Neue Bach-Ausgabe].* Series 1–8. Kassel: Bärenreiter, 1954– .

Notes   *Music Library Association Notes* (1943–)

PurcellW   *The Works of Henry Purcell.* 32 v. London: Novello, 1878–1965. Second ed. London: Novello, 1961– .

Quantz   Johann Joachim Quantz, *On Playing the Flute,* trans. Edward R. Reilly, second ed. (New York: Schirmer, 1985).

RdeM   *Revue de musicologie* (1917–)

Recherches	*Recherches sur la musique classique française* (1960–)
Rowen	Rowen, Ruth Halle. *Music through Sources and Documents.* Englewood Cliffs, New Jersey: Prentice-Hall, 1979.
RV	Ryom, P. *Verzeichnis der Werke Antonio Vivaldis: kleine Ausgabe.* Leipzig: Deutscher Verlag für Musik, 1974.
SchützW	*Neue Ausgabe sämtlicher Werke.* Kassel: Bärenreiter, 1953–1971.
SIMG	*Sammelbände der Internationalen Musik-Gesellschaft* (1899–1914)
Strunk	Strunk, Oliver. *Source Readings in Music History from Classical Antiquity through the Romantic Era.* New York: Norton, 1950.
VivaldiW	*Le opere di Antonio Vivaldi.* Ed. Gian Francesco Malipiero. N.p.: Ricordi, 1947– .

Preface

The aim of this book is to introduce listeners and performers to important issues of baroque performance practice, issues that arise whenever baroque music is played or sung. It is a guide to applying the principles of interpretation in different performing situations and in different types of music. My approach is selective but wide ranging, with musical examples and references to musical works drawn from a variety of genres, both vocal and instrumental.

Scores for eleven works are included for close study of entire movements that illustrate critical concepts. Many of the scores are reproduced in facsimile to help performers become familiar with different conventions of seventeenth- and eighteenth-century notation. The cassette tape, available as a companion to this book, contains recent performances of the same pieces by soloists and groups of international reputation. (For contents, see Appendix A.) I have chosen the performances with a view toward representing both the diversity and individuality of early music groups. Together the scores and recorded performances add a broader aural experience to the study of performance practice and demonstrate how some issues may be solved in actual performing situations.

The literature on the performance practices of baroque music has grown to vast proportions within the past three decades. Many excellent books document specific issues, and facsimile editions of treatises are readily available for study. Because such a wealth of information is now available as reference material, there is a need for a concise guide to the subject, one that identifies performance practice issues and guides the reader toward further investigation and interpretation of the evidence, not only through the treatises of the baroque era, but also through evidence in the music itself.

This book differs from existing studies of baroque interpretation in its practical approach which relates information in the treatises to appropriate musical examples, and in its emphasis upon the close study of selected musical scores (in Appendix A) in conjunction with the text. It is intended to be used as a guide for listeners and performers who have some familiarity with baroque music, and as a textbook for undergraduate and graduate courses in baroque performance practice. The bibliographical notes at the end of each chapter lead the interested reader to further research on each issue. A general bibliography can be found in Appendix B, and Appendix C contains a list of pre-1800 sources cited in this book. Footnotes to the text, located at the end of each chapter, cite specific modern editions or pages from a particular treatise; whenever an author or treatise is mentioned without a footnote, a full reference can be found in Appendix C under the author's name.

Most of us approach the subject with a desire to translate knowledge of early performing techniques into aural experience, either through listening or performance. These needs can perhaps best be met initially by a study of the issues that relate most directly to the sound and interpretation of the music. In studying historical performance practices, we are attempting to define both the boundaries and the freedom that were inherent in baroque performing techniques. Within a limited time frame, such as a university semester, most students find it impossible to assimilate fully the techniques of baroque performance on an instrument, but I hope that this guide will provide the starting point for more detailed study of individual instruments, their repertories, and performing techniques.

Chapter 1 introduces the field of performance practice and its goals, the limits of authenticity, and characteristics of baroque sound. Chapters 2 to 8 attempt to define and illustrate some of the issues one encounters when performing baroque music: tempo, dynamics, pitch and temperament, the basso continuo, articulation, rhythm and notational conventions, and appropriate ornamentation. Readers may select topics in any order because the chapters are self-contained; instructors may expand or omit material as the need arises.

In this venture our broader awareness of baroque performing techniques, sought through the exploration of different approaches, should move us closer to the goal of studying early performance practices: a convincing and moving performance.

Acknowledgments

Many colleagues and students contributed in valuable ways during the preparation of this book. Some material was first developed for a workbook on baroque performance practice, which was supported by a grant in 1983 from the Centre for Teaching and Learning at McGill University. Lise Viens and Andrew Couse, both graduate students, were able assistants toward the completion of that project, and Robert Mundle assisted me in many ways with the present manuscript. Several colleagues kindly offered encouragement and thoughtful criticisms of the book in various drafts, among whom Sandra Mangsen (University of Western Ontario), Paul Pedersen (University of Toronto), and Newman Powell (Valparaiso, Indiana) deserve special thanks. Alan Curtis provided encouragement of another sort through his exemplary performances and scholarship.

For guidance at every step during the book's production, I am grateful to the staff of Amadeus Press. Dr. Reinhard G. Pauly's discerning judgment resulted in many improvements, and Karen Kirtley efficiently solved many problems associated with the illustrations and cassette tape. I am particularly indebted to Eve S. Goodman for her adept editorial work that clarified numerous passages of my prose.

Thanks are due also to Cynthia Leive (head librarian), John Black, David Curtis, and the staff of the Marvin Duchow Music Library at McGill University, to whom I turned repeatedly for guidance with bibliographic matters. I am grateful to the Faculty of Music at McGill for permitting the use of its recording studio to prepare the cassette tape, and to McGill Records for permission to use a recording from its catalogue without a fee. Finally, my students have been a continuing source of enthusiasm and support, and it is to them that this book is dedicated.

PERFORMING BAROQUE MUSIC

1

Performance Practice and Baroque Sound

Musical notation by its very nature is inexact. The symbols represent merely an approximation of the duration, volume, pitch, and rhythm of musical sounds. Some features, such as how an instrument is tuned or the pitch at which it plays, are taken for granted and may not figure in the notation at all. Others belong to style or convention and may not be explicit, such as the length of a fermata or the pauses between movements. Performers must rely to a considerable extent upon experience and intuition whenever they transfer music from notation into sound, for much is left to the individual's discretion. Many composers of the twentieth century have attempted to indicate their intentions more precisely than composers of the past did, but the performer still has much to interpret.

To perform music of any age or culture, we must be able to identify the traditions and conventions that belong to it. Performers use this knowledge to provide a stylistic context within which a personal interpretation of the music develops. The farther back in time one goes, the greater are the difficulties in interpreting the notation, not only because aspects of the symbols may be imprecise, but also because the meanings of some marks have changed through centuries of use. By recognizing features common to music composed in a given period, in a particular place, or by an individual composer, we can begin to define the stylistic characteristics that help us interpret the notation. If we are successful, this knowledge eventually becomes part of our intuitive perception of style. Without it, the musical language of the past would lose its subtle shades of meaning and expression.

If we seek to perform music as we think the composer imagined it would sound, we must embark upon the study of performance practice. This ever-widening field attempts to interpret the written musical document and to create an appropriate sound based upon that interpretation. The materials for the study of performance practice therefore reach beyond the music itself. The task is similar in some ways to that of the restorer of a painting, who painstakingly recreates colors, shades, and textures that were changed or lost over time.

The field of performance practice, or *Aufführungspraxis*, is only about a century old. Early investigators such as Arnold Schering (1877–1941) and Hugo Goldschmidt (1859–1920) documented important repertories and studied how their notations are to be interpreted. These writers were among the first, since the eighteenth century, to discuss authentic interpretations of the figured bass, dynamics, and ornamentation, and to identify the types of indications that are often missing from baroque scores, such as instrumentation.

Recreating a correct musical text became the first aim of performance practice, and from the middle of the nineteenth century onward, the monumental collected editions of major baroque figures were issued: the Bach-Gesellschaft in 1851, and those for Handel (1858), Purcell (1878), Schütz (1885), Rameau (1895), and Monteverdi (1926). In general, the editors presented the works in these volumes with few emendations and retained the original note values, ornaments, and other aspects of the notation. Some editions also include comments about the physical appearance of the sources, but usually the performer has little opportunity to study the variants in different sources, since the editors present only one reading. More recent editorial thought has moved toward providing as much information from the extant sources as possible, either in the edition itself or in supplementary critical notes. Given access to such information from the original manuscripts and prints, one can study the evidence, review the editor's choice, and consider the various possibilities. New collected editions, such as the *Neue Bach Ausgabe* (1954-) and the *Hallische Händel-Ausgabe* (1955-), include critical commentaries with information about chronology, performance matters, and a list of variants for each work. These editions are still underway, and others have begun more recently, such as those for Buxtehude, Lully, and Rameau. For some composers, such as Marais, Telemann, and Vivaldi, a significant number of instrumental works has been published, but a comparatively small amount of their vocal music is available. Much editorial work, therefore, still remains to be done.

With the efforts of Arnold Dolmetsch (1858–1940) and others, the music also began to be heard once again using old instruments. Along with increasing interest in historical performance came new questions and problems of interpretation. Research into the playing techniques of early instruments and the design of the instruments themselves has raised an important new issue, that of authenticity. As a concept, authenticity can have several meanings. We can speak of an authentic source as one whose attribution is not in question, or as one that is known to originate with the composer, and is not a version or arrangement by someone else. When applied to musical performance, authenticity may be regarded as an attempt to perform within a context of historical faithfulness, either by adhering closely to the composer's wishes (if they are known), or by considering the conventions and historical circumstances of performances associated with the composer. Because it carries the connotation of "right" or "correct," however, the word *authentic* is sometimes mistakenly regarded as a way of limiting the boundaries within which good performances may fall. A historically informed approach should have the opposite effect; it may even expand the interpretive boundaries for modern performers by leading them to explore techniques no longer in use today.

If performance practice seeks to recreate the music as the composer wanted it to sound, should our goal be authentic performance? Although a performer may look for some authentic solutions to the problems of interpretation, one cannot usually achieve a fully authentic performance for at least two reasons. First, circumstances for a composer were rarely ideal, and baroque composers often based their choices upon the particular performers available to them and may even have been forced to alter their conception of a piece because of a given set of circumstances. Second, we cannot attempt merely to recreate musical performances as they were in the seventeenth or eighteenth centuries. Our concerts are events of the twentieth century, and it is rare that a totally authentic performance can even be attempted. Nevertheless, the study of such factors as the original size and balance of an instrumental group or choir may help us to understand certain stylistic features of the music and how its notation can be interpreted.

Our study of baroque performance practice will therefore focus upon the written evidence in the musical document as well as the many unwritten conventions and styles which contribute to interpretation. Performance practice has broadened today to encompass all music of the past and to bring scholars and performers together in search of a common goal: to understand the composer's intentions as they have come down to us in musical manuscripts and other documents, and to direct our knowledge toward an effective and enjoyable performance. In seeking answers to the problems of performance practice, we are attempting to define not the single authentic performance but the boundaries within which good performances fall. A primary aim in any performance is to interpret the music in a moving or expressive manner; authenticity is not a goal but a means to this end.

The role of the performer in baroque music

Musical performance, having as its aim a moving or enjoyable communication to an audience, has two elements: the musical score (the actual document, usually written down in some form), and the performer's interpretation. The balance between these two elements varies greatly in different centuries and even with different composers. In the baroque period, the performer's interpretation was considered at least as important as the written score, and in many cases it was considered more important. It is easy to see, then, why musical scores from the period do not provide all the indications that belong to the creative responsibility of the performer, such as slurs or articulations, dynamics, and ornamentation.

Since performance practices varied according to place, time, and individual circumstances, we may well ask whether it will be possible to study them together as "baroque," even though they are spread over more than a century and separated geographically. There will be some common elements in baroque interpretation which, though not bounded firmly by the dates 1600 and 1750, do make it possible to consider the period as a whole. These common elements can be traced to three important characteristics of musical interpretation during this period: (1) the importance of the voice as a model for instrumental performance, (2) the significance of the words and their expressive delivery in all types of music, and (3) the use of a basso continuo in nearly all ensembles as a foundation or harmonic support. Because these features are common to most baroque music, some matters of interpretation will remain constant as well, while other conventions will change according to the demands of individual composers and musical characteristics.

The sources and tools for studying baroque performance

The tools for the study of baroque performance practice are numerous, and it is important to consider as many different ones as possible when studying a particular style or notation. If one is using a modern edition, the task will be to identify its sources and determine how closely they may reflect the composer's intentions. The first, and perhaps most important, document is the composer's own score, if available, or other manuscripts and early printed editions. If we do not have the composer's autograph, we may have to accept one or more other sources as the best surviving copies. Usually the most important sources will be the ones that can be traced most closely to the composer's family or pupils, or to a somewhat wider circle including a known copyist or a particular geographical region.

Other tools that may aid the study of performance practices are treatises or instruction books on how to play early instruments, and theoretical works on composition and harmony. Peripheral types of written documents that may prove useful are concert reviews, memoirs, payment lists, libretti, and the like. Visual documents, such as engravings, drawings, and paintings may help to explain or confirm other written evidence and may be particularly helpful in documenting playing techniques. Finally, the instruments themselves can provide us with considerable information about timbre and balance in the baroque ensemble.

Baroque sound

In attempting to play or listen to baroque music, one usually begins with a concern for the sound, a feature by no means easily described, but nevertheless a crucial one as a basis upon which to build other matters of style. As a result of the opportunity to hear performances on both modern and baroque instruments— obviously, an opportunity that eighteenth-century musicians never had!—we are often tempted to compare them. In applying descriptive appellations to the differences we hear, some listeners may observe that, for example, the baroque violin has a thinner, more penetrating sound than its modern counterpart, whose tone to our accustomed ear is full and warm. Many writers and listeners have fallen into the trap of evaluating early instruments in terms of their ability to measure up to modern standards of volume, tone quality, and technical requirements. The underlying assumption of this approach is that instruments have undergone gradual improvements toward their current state of perfection. An evolutionary concept of history, however, is fraught with misconceptions. A more fruitful evaluation would be based upon a comparison of an instrument's characteristics with the demands of the music written expressly for it, by determining how it was able to realize the performance practices in use when that music was played.

Musicians studying performance practice must take care not to let twentieth-century expectations influence their views of early practices, but instead attempt to study these early techniques in relation to the music written for them. The characteristics of the instruments themselves tend to contribute to the musical style of a composition, and the instruments are therefore an essential part of the study of performance practices for any musical repertory. Singers, too, may find that instruments provide valuable clues about the variety of tone color and types of articulation appropriate to baroque music. The changes in construction that many instruments underwent during the late eighteenth and early nineteenth centuries allowed some the ability to play more evenly. Woodwind instruments were able to manage chromatic passages easily and rapidly. String instruments gained more power, and smoother connections between strokes became possible with the longer, heavier bow designed by François Tourte (and still in use today). But with these gains also went some losses. The one-keyed baroque flute played in certain keys with difficulty, but it possessed a natural shading of sound in which some notes of a scale sounded clear and open while others were more shaded or "covered" in sound. This produced a characteristically nuanced sound even in a passage of stepwise notes, and different registers on the instrument also had different dynamic characteristics. Notes in the lower octave, especially from d^1 to a^1, were soft by comparison with notes above g^2, which were more brilliant. When stepwise notes were played on the instrument, some sounded open and clear, while others were more muted and closed. The *flattement*, or finger vibrato, was possible only on woodwind instruments with few keys or only one key. This ornament therefore cannot be produced on the modern flute or oboe. The balance and texture of baroque music incorporates the natural tonal characteristics of early instruments, and to replace them may cause performers to alter features of the music unknowingly.

Some characteristics of baroque sound can be studied in the forlana (Appendix A) from André Campra's *opéra-ballet, L'Europe galante* (1697). In contrast to modern scores, in which one would usually find a part for each instrument in the orchestra, French scores of the late seventeenth and early eighteenth centuries often combine several instruments on a single staff. The word *tous* (everyone) at the beginning indicates that the strings and woodwinds (oboes and bassoons) play until the passage marked *hautbois* and *bassons*, where the strings drop out. Except for the trio passages for the oboes and bassoons, the two upper parts are in unison throughout. Thus the texture is predominantly in five parts, but the doubling of the outer parts with woodwinds gives them prominence, while the three inner parts are played by strings alone. The baroque woodwinds, being generally softer than their modern counterparts and made of wood, blend quite naturally with the violins. In this forlana, as in much orchestral music of the baroque era, the woodwinds double the upper and lower strings, producing a single, blended tone color for each line, which in turn contributes to the overall balance. Other characteristics of the sound when played on period instruments include a contrast of timbre and dynamic level when the full orchestra is reduced to a trio texture (mm. 17–20, 29–32, 37–40) featuring the woodwinds alone. The metrical accentuation and the dynamic nuances that can be heard on long notes also belong to the realm of baroque sound; all of these features will be studied in greater detail in subsequent chapters.

Bibliographical notes

A valuable survey of the field, its history, and goals, is the article "Performing Practice," by Howard Mayer Brown, James W. McKinnon, and Robert Winter in *GroveInstr*; see also "Editing" and "Historical Editions" in *Grove*. The latter includes a list of critical editions for individual composers and individual repertories. Appendix B contains a list of bibliographies of performance practice, and a list of pre-1800 sources cited in this book can be found in Appendix C.

Differences between modern and baroque string instruments are discussed by Jaap Schröder and Christopher Hogwood. For an introduction to issues raised in singing early music, see Antony Ransome's article.

Detailed information on instruments, singing style, and several specific issues (including pitch, tuning, and keyboard fingering) can be found in *Performance Practice: Music after 1600*, edited by Howard Mayer Brown and Stanley Sadie. An informative, brief discussion of major issues in performance practice can be found in Robert Donington's article on instruments in baroque music, an excerpt from his *Performer's Guide to Baroque Music*. Two other major works by Donington, both indispensable for the study of performance practice, are also listed below.

The degree to which authenticity can and should be the goal of musical performance has been the subject of numerous essays. A pioneering study, still valuable today, is that of Putnam Aldrich. Jeremy Montagu argues for the necessity of using exact copies of old instruments. The controversy was refuelled by Richard Taruskin, Daniel Leech-Wilkinson, Nicholas Temperley, and Robert Winter in "The Limits of Authenticity," and in chapter 6 of Joseph Kerman's *Contemplating Music: Challenges to Musicology*, in which he discusses the relationship between performance practice and the field of musicology. Opinions on various sides of the issue are collected in *Authenticity and Early Music, a Symposium*, where fascinating, if polemical, differences of opinion abound.

FOR FURTHER STUDY

Aldrich, Putnam. "The 'Authentic' Performance of Baroque Music." In *Essays on Music in Honor of Archibald T. Davison*, 161–171. Cambridge: Harvard University, Department of Music, 1957.

Brown, Howard Mayer, and Stanley Sadie, editors. *Performance Practice: Music after 1600*. New York and London: W. W. Norton and Co., 1989.

Camesi, David. "Eighteenth-Century Conducting Practices." *JRME* 18 (1970): 365–376.

Donington, Robert. *A Performer's Guide to Baroque Music*. New York: Charles Scribner's Sons, 1973.

_____ . *Baroque Music: Style and Performance*. London: Faber Music, 1982.

_____ . "The Choice of Instruments in Baroque Music." *EM* 1 (July 1973): 131–138.

_____ . *The Interpretation of Early Music, New Version*. London: Faber, 1974.

_____ . "The Present Position of Authenticity." *Performance Practice Review* 2 (Fall 1989): 117–125.

Dreyfus, Laurence. "Early Music Defended Against Its Devotees: a Theory of Historical Performance in the Twentieth Century." *MQ* 69 (1983): 297–322.

Ecorcheville, Jules. "Les textes de musique ancienne et leurs reéditions modernes." *Mercure musical et bulletin français de la société internationale de musicologie* 6 (June 1907): 626–635.

Fortune, Nigel. "Italian 17th-Century Singing." *ML* 35 (1954): 206–219.

Grout, Donald J. "On Historical Authenticity in the Performance of Old Music." In *Essays in Honor of Archibald T. Davison by His Associates*, 341–347. Cambridge: Harvard University, Department of Music, 1957.

Haas, Robert. *Aufführungspraxis der Musik*. Potsdam: Wildpark, 1931.

Kenyon, Nicholas, ed. *Authenticity and Early Music, a Symposium*. Oxford: Oxford University Press, 1988.

Kerman, Joseph. "The Historical Performance Movement." In *Contemplating Music: Challenges to Musicology*, 183–217. Cambridge, MA: Harvard University Press, 1985.

Leppard, Raymond. *Authenticity in Music*. London: Faber Music, 1988. Portland, OR: Amadeus, 1988.

Mertin, Josef. *Alte Musik: Wege zur Aufführungspraxis*. Vienna: E. Lafite, 1978. Transl. Siegmund Levarie as *Early Music: Approaches to Performance Practice*. New York: Da Capo, 1986.

Montagu, Jeremy. "The 'Authentic' Sound of Early Music." *EM* 3 (July 1975): 242–243.

Nathan, Hans. "The Sense of History in Musical Interpretation." *MR* 13 (May 1952): 85–100.

Neumann, Frederick. "The Use of Baroque Treatises on Musical Performance." *ML* 48 (1967): 315–324.

Pincherle, Marc. "On the Rights of the Interpreter in the Performance of Seventeenth- and Eighteenth-Century Music." *MQ* 44 (April 1958): 145–166.

Rangel-Ribeiro, Victor. *Baroque Music: a Practical Guide for the Performer*. New York: Schirmer, 1981.

Ransome, Antony. "Towards an Authentic Vocal Style and Technique in Late Baroque Performance." *EM* 6 (July 1978): 417–419.

Schering, Arnold. "Zur instrumentalen Verzierungskunst im 18. Jahrhundert." *SIMG* 7 (1905–1906): 365–385.

_____ . *Aufführungspraxis alter Musik*. Leipzig: Quelle and Meyer, 1931.

Schröder, Jaap, and Christopher Hogwood. "The Developing Violin." *EM* 7 (April 1979): 155–165.

Stevens, Denis. "Performance Practice in Baroque Vocal Music." *CMS* 18 (1978): 9–19.

[Symposium] "Performance Practice in the 17th and 18th Centuries." In *International*

Musicological Society: Report of the Eighth Congress, New York 1961, 220–235. Kassel: Bärenreiter, 1961.

Taruskin, Richard, with Daniel Leech-Wilkinson, Nicholas Temperley, and Robert Winter. "The Limits of Authenticity." *EM* 12 (February 1984): 3–25.

Westrup, Jack A. "Monteverdi and the Orchestra." *ML* 21 (1940): 230–245.

Wynne, Shirley. "Baroque Manners and Passions in Modern Performance." In *Opera and Vivaldi,* ed. Michael Collins and Elise K. Kirk, 170–178. Austin: University of Texas Press, 1984.

2

Tempo and Spirit

The tempo of a piece refers literally to the time in which it is performed, or more specifically to its measure, beat, or pulse. Tempo implies a steadiness of beat, usually measured in beats per minute. Certain types of pieces may be described as without tempo, such as recitatives or cadenzas, and in this sense the mark *a tempo* signifies a return or taking up again of a steady pulse. Of course, even a regular speed is understood to be relative and affected by minor fluctuations according to the demands of the music and the interpretation of the artist.

The earliest method of measuring tempo was the human pulse. During the baroque era, theorists still regarded it as the simplest form of measuring speed, but several other experimental methods were also devised. Thomas Mace (1676) was first to describe the use of a pendulum for keeping time,[1] and several later theorists refined the method by shortening or lengthening the pendulum in order to regulate the speed. Most of these experiments were short-lived, largely because the pendulum was too awkward to use. It was not until 1816 that Johann Nepomuk Maelzel manufactured the metronome, a mechanical device small enough to be practical for an individual player, with a compound pendulum calibrated with the number of beats per minute.

Although the metronome is certainly a useful tool, few performers would wish to adopt a speed that is entirely regulated by it. Several composers, including Beethoven and Brahms, left precise metronome markings for certain pieces, but these marks were often changed at a later time or ignored by the composer himself, and they do not necessarily form a reliable measure of speed for modern performances.

Tempo is affected by many factors, such as the size and acoustical characteristics of the hall, the particular instruments being used, the size of the ensemble, and even how one feels at the time. Thus, when we speak of establishing a correct tempo for a piece, it is understood that a given speed will allow minor adjustment according to the circumstances of individual performances.

Tempo mark and meter in baroque music

Early in the baroque era, the speed of a piece or movement was not usually indicated with a tempo mark, because it was implied to a considerable extent by the meter. Proportional relationships between meters often governed the tempos of sections within pieces, as they had in earlier times. In renaissance music the beat was regulated by an up-and-down motion of the hand, called the tactus. According to Gaffurius (1496), the speed of the tactus was equal to the pulse of a person who is breathing normally. Within the notational system, this relatively constant tactus was represented with proportional relationships between meters, so that one note value (that of the tactus) remained constant throughout the sections of a piece, no matter how the meter changed. Residual traces of this practice can still be found in baroque music, as in Monteverdi's use of the signature O3 or Ø3 as a triple meter, with three semibreves (whole notes) per measure, as in "Ardo avvampo" and "Ogni amante è guerrier," from *Madrigali Guerrieri et Amorosi* (Venice, 1638).[2] The original notation is somewhat confusing to performers today, and for this reason, editors sometimes reduce the original note values to quarter notes in 3/4. In determining a tempo, however, modern players will do well to ascertain the original meter and note values, for they may provide a clue both to the tempo and how it changes within the piece. Both the "cut O" (Φ) and the "cut C" (₵) were used to indicate diminution, or a performance at a faster than usual speed, in early baroque music. The difference between ₵ and C was not necessarily fixed by a 2:1 ratio; ₵ was sometimes one-third faster than C.

Tempo marks did not appear with any regularity until the old proportional notation system was in its decline. Its gradual breakdown was more or less complete by about the end of the seventeenth century. That tempo marks came to be a reliable indication of the spirit of the piece can be seen in Sebastien de Brossard's explanation of "cut C" in his article on tempo [*temps*] from his *Dictionaire de musique* (Paris, 1703):

> The "cut C" is found turned from left to right thus ₵, or from right to left thus Ɔ. When it is to the *right* the Italians still call it *Tempo alla breve*, because formerly under this sign all the notes were performed in diminution by half of their value; but at present it denotes only that one must beat time *slowly in 2*, or *very quickly in 4* [*à deux temps graves, ou à quatre temps fort vîtes*]; unless it is marked *Largo, Adagio, Lento,* or some mark that warns that one must beat time *very slowly*. And when one sees with this sign the words *da Capella*, and *alla breve*, it denotes *in 2 very fast* [*deux temps tres-vîtes*]. It means this also when the sign is reversed, but one rarely finds it thus (Brossard, 154).

Determining the appropriate spirit

In baroque music, tempo marks serve several different purposes and do not necessarily refer only to the speed at which one performs the music. Frequently they indicate a mood or spirit of expression that suits the music. Thus the word *allegro* in baroque music implies "cheerfully" (but not necessarily fast), and *largo* "in a grand, singing manner" (but not necessarily slow). French writers used the word *mouvement* to speak of the spirit a composition required.

In the eighteenth century the spirit was frequently described as the "affect" present in a piece or movement. The word *affect* implied more than the present-day word *emotion* does; rather the baroque concept of affect was deeply rooted in the belief in the soul exerting control over the body and filling it with passions that are strongly expressed. In the foreword to his *Madrigali guerrieri et amorosi* (Venice, 1638), Monteverdi cites three "principal passions or affections of our mind . . . namely, anger [*ira*], moderation [*temperenzio*], and humility or supplication [*supplicatione*]."[3] These three passions correspond to three types of musical expression for Monteverdi: agitated [*concitato*], soft [*molle*], and moderate [*temperato*]. Most of the seven passions named by Quantz (1752) could be described today as feelings or moods: boldness, flattery, gaiety or liveliness, melancholy (tenderness), majesty (the sublime), the pathetic, and the serious. Other eighteenth-century writers such as Geminiani and Mattheson observed many more passions (up to sixty-five!) than Quantz, who may have restricted the number because of his desire to identify the musical character of each and its appropriate articulation on the flute.

According to many baroque theorists, the key in which a composition was written also contributed significantly to its affect. A comparison of the attributes of the major and minor keys according to five seventeenth- and eighteenth-century writers is shown in Table 2-1. Even though LaBorde's comments date from 1780, he cites many examples from Rameau's operas to illustrate the character of various keys, and it therefore seems appropriate to consider his descriptions alongside those of earlier writers. We should remember, however, that a key's attributes depend upon the temperament of the instruments and also upon the sonorities of the particular instruments being used. A key such as A major may bring forth strong, bright sonorities from the violins because of the available open strings, but the sharps produce some covered sounds and intonation difficulties for the flute and oboe. Nor were pitch levels uniform in the baroque era, making comparison of absolute pitches virtually impossible. Nevertheless, it is apparent that consideration of key characteristics did influence both composers and performers in many cases, and the key was one of many features that contributed to the spirit or affect of a piece.

Table 2-1. Major and minor keys and their attributes, according to Charpentier, Mattheson, Rameau, Quantz, and LaBorde.

Key and Mode	Marc-Antoine Charpentier, *Règles de composition* (ca. 1682), manuscript, Paris, Bibliothèque Nationale, nouv. acq. 6355	Johann Mattheson, *Das neu-eröffnete Orchestre* (1713)	Jean-Philippe Rameau, *Traité de l'harmonie* (Paris, 1722), 164	Johann Joachimm Quantz, *On Playing the Flute* (1752), 164–165	Jean Benjamin de LaBorde, *Essai sur la musique ancienne et moderne* (Paris, 1780), 28–29
C major	"gay and warlike"	"rude and impudent character; suited to rejoicing"	"songs of mirth and rejoicing"		"serious, grave, majestic, suited to war, sometimes for religious subjects" [both modes]
C minor	"obscure and sad"	"extremely lovely, but sad"	"tenderness and plaints"	"melancholy . . . mournful"	
D major	"joyous and very warlike"	"somewhat shrill and stubborn; suited to noisy, joyful, warlike, and rousing things"	"songs of mirth and rejoicing"		"ardent, proud, impetuous, vehement, terrible; sometimes also more quiet"
D minor	"serious and pious"	"somewhat devoit, calm, also somewhat grand, pleasant, and expressive of contentment"	"sweetness and tenderness"		
E flat major	"cruel and hard"	"pathetic; concerned with serious and plaintive things; bitterly hostile to all lasciviousness"			"grave and very somber"
E major	"quarrelsome and boisterous"	"expresses a desperate or wholly fatal sadness incomparably well; most suited for the extremes of helpless and hopeless love"	"tender and gay songs; grandeur and magnificence"		"animated, rousing, sometimes pathetic and proper for softness [*mollesse*]" [both modes]
E minor	"effeminate, amorous, plaintive"	"hardly joyful because it is normally	"sweetness and tenderness"		

"very pensive, profound, grieved, and sad, [but] still hope for consolation"

Key				
F major	"furious and quick-tempered subjects"	"capable of expressing the most beautiful sentiments in the world in a natural way and with incomparable facility, politeness, and cleverness"	"tempests, furies, and the like"	"noisy, but sometimes melancholy and pathetic"
F minor	"obscure and plaintive"	"mild and calm, deep and heavy with despair, exceedingly moving; sometimes causes the listener to shudder with horror"	"tenderness and plaints"	"melancholy . . . mournful"
G major	"quietly joyful"	"possesses much that is insinuating and persuasive; quite brilliant, suited to serious and to cheerful things"	"tender and gay songs"	"affectionate, but gay, often soft [doux] and majestic" [both modes]
G minor	"serious and magnificent"	"almost the most beautiful key; combines a serious quality with spirited loveliness, also brings an uncommon grace and kindness"	"sweetness and tenderness"	"melancholy . . . mournful"
A major	"joyful and pastoral"	"very gripping, although at the same time brilliant, more suited to lamenting and sad passions than to divertissements; especially good for violin music."	"songs of mirth and rejoicing; grandeur and magnificence"	"brilliant and sometimes calm and peaceful" [moth modes]

Table 2-1. Continued.

Key and Mode	Marc-Antoine Charpentier, *Règles de composition* (ca. 1682), manuscript, Paris, Bibliothèque Nationale, nouv. acq. 6355	Johann Mattheson, *Das neu-eröffnete Orchestre* (1713)	Jean-Philippe Rameau, *Traité de l'harmonie* (Paris, 1722), 164	Johann Joachimm Quantz, *On Playing the Flute* (1752), 164–165	Jean Benjamin de LaBorde, *Essai sur la musique ancienne et moderne* (Paris, 1780), 28–29
A minor	"tender and plaintive"	"somewhat plaintive, melancholy, honorable, and calm"		"melancholy . . . mournful"	
B major	"harsh and plaintive"	"occurs only sometimes, seems to have an offensive, hard, unpleasant, and also somewhat desperate character"			"animated and brilliant; sometimes agreeable and soft, other times given to funereal airs and sublime meditations" [both modes]
B minor	"solitary, melancholic"	"it can touch the heart"			
B flat major	"magnificent and joyful"	"very diverting and sumptuous, also somewhat modest, can pass as both magnificent and dainty"	"tempests, furies, and like subjects"		"imposing, although sad" [both modes]
B flat minor	"obscure and terrible"		"mournful songs"		

Sources appear under the author's name in Appendix C. A facsimile of Charpentier's manuscript is included in Lillian M. Ruff, "M.-A. Charpentier's 'Règles de composition,'" in *The Consort* 24 (1967), 251. Mattheson's descriptions are condensed from Rita Steblin, in *A History of Key Characteristics in the Eighteenth and Early Nineteenth Centuries*, UMI Studies in Musicology no. 67 (UMI Research Press: Ann Arbor, 1983), 222–308. The passages are given in the original language on pp. 309–315. Translations of passages from Charpentier, Rameau, and LaBorde are mine.

Affect and the aria

The composition that adhered most clearly to an expression of a single affect was the da capo aria. Although its language was often couched in simile and metaphor, the aria text set forth one affect whose expression could be intensified through its musical setting. Mattheson and others describe the aria as a composition in two parts which "concisely expresses a great affection,"[4] that is, a single affect. After 1740 or thereabouts, some arias and movements of instrumental pieces do express two or more contrasting affects which may even be marked by a change of tempo and key within the piece. Such compositions were associated with the new *galant* style to which Quantz's description of alternating passions also belongs.

Charles de Brosses offers descriptions of three types of Italian arias he heard during his travels through Italy in 1739 and 1740.[5] The first type, written for powerful voices and allowing the most ornamentation, featured a comparison in the text between the singer's feelings and "an agitated sea, impetuous wind, a lion pursued by hunters, or the horror of a still night." In such an aria, wind instruments (oboe, trumpet, or horns) were often used. The second type, according to de Brosses, for fine, flexible voices, contained delicate thoughts or comparisons with gentle, agreeable things, such as zephyrs, birds, murmuring brooks, or pastoral life. This type of air has a "flattering nature" and may be similar to a menuet or musette. The third type is "passionate, tender, and touching," and expresses heartfelt sentiment. Here ornamentation is not appropriate, according to de Brosses, and the singer should instead render the aria simply and expressively.

Since each character usually sang several arias within an entire *opera seria*, the audience heard contrasting facets of each character's personality and feelings as events unfolded. An example of de Brosse's first type is Vitige's aria, "Sirti, scogli, tempeste" from the third act of Handel's *Flavio* (Appendix A). Although Vitige is a male courtier, his role was written for the soprano Margherita Durastanti and first performed by her in 1723. For this aria, Vitige is alone following a scene in which the King, Flavio, pursues the lovely Teodata, whom Vitige loves. The text of Vitige's aria, written by Nicola Haym, metaphorically speaks of Vitige's jealousy of Flavio's interest in Teodata as an obstacle to smooth sailing in the sea of love. Its two sentences each contain three lines of ten, six, and five syllables:

Sirti, scogli, tempeste, procelle	Sandbanks, rocks, tempests, storms
m'additan le stelle	are what the stars point to
nel mare d'amor.	in the sea of love.
Tante sono l'acerbe mie pene	So bitter are my woes that,
che incerto de spene	uncertain whether there is hope,
m'opprime il dolor.	grief is a burden to me.

Handel sets the text as a da capo aria, with the first three lines of text as the A section (mm. 1–40) and the last three lines as the B section (mm. 41–50). It begins in G minor with a bold leaping gesture from the violins and oboes in unison, followed by a contrasting chromatic motive and a fury of sixteenth notes. The B section shifts toward the relative major and D minor for Vitige's more intense expression of grief. Although no tempo mark is present in Handel's score, a lively tempo is assured by the agitated melody and bass line, intensifying the metaphorical anger expressed in the text.[6]

Determining the appropriate spirit of a baroque composition is more important than setting its speed, for without the former, even the "right" tempo will not draw the appropriate expression from a piece. For this decision, the music itself usually provides most of the necessary clues about spirit, including such features as the meter, text, key, harmonic rhythm, amount of dissonance, ornamentation, and sometimes the note values themselves. Tempo marks are frequently absent, especially in vocal music, but even when they are present we must consider them along with other musical features in order to arrive at an appropriate spirit and tempo for a piece. In the subsequent discussion, several examples will illustrate how this can be done.

Tempo in seventeenth-century music

Monteverdi provides a few specific directions for the organist concerning tempo in his *Magnificat a 7*. In the continuo part of "Suscepit Israel," he indicates "Principal alone [the desired organ registration], which is played *adaggio* (sic) because the two sopranos sing in echo [i.e., imitation]." For "Quia fecit" he indicates "Principal alone, which is played *adaggio* because the vocal and instrumental parts have eighth- and sixteenth-note motion." He uses the word *tardo*, meaning slower, in a similar harmonic context in "Et exultavit," and both *adaggio* and *tardo* appear to be a warning not to play so fast as to obscure the moving parts or the echo interplay of the soloists.[7]

Heinrich Schütz (1585–1672) also used the word *tardo* (or *tarde*) on occasion. In two works entitled "Gib unsern Fürsten" and "Verleih uns Frieden," from his *Symphoniae Sacrae II* (Dresden, 1647), the sections marked *tarde* are in Common time (C) and follow a Presto section (6/4 or 3/2).[8] In both cases performers would slow the speed at the change of meter because of the word *tarde*. The term evidently retained its meaning for some time, as can be seen from Brossard's *Dictionaire* (1703), in which *tardo* is described as "slow" [*lente*], meaning that "one must keep time gravely, sadly, slowly, in a slurred manner" (Brossard, 149–150).

Even when tempo marks are lacking, as in many seventeenth-century works, a section with prominent dissonance, chromaticism, or many changes of harmony may require a relatively slow tempo, whereas imitative or dancelike sections are often more spirited and lively. Henry Purcell (1659–1695) employed the English words "brisk" or "drag" as well as "slow" and "quick" in his fantasias for viols (1680).[9] In Fantasia No. 1 for four viols, a "brisk" section is lively and imitative with predominantly eighth-note motion, whereas a section marked "drag" is polyphonic and has a more dissonant and chromatic harmony. In Purcell's twelve *Sonatas of 3 Parts* (London, 1683) the composer included a reference to tempo in his address "to the Reader."[10] He acknowledges his debt to Italian instrumental writing by stating that "he has faithfully endeavour'd a just imitation of the most fam'd Italian masters," and he offers the following advice for performers concerning tempo:

> It remains only that the English Practitioner be enform'd, that he will find a few terms of Art perhaps unusual to him, the chief of which are the following: *Adagio* and *Grave*, which import nothing but a very slow movement: *Presto Largo, Poco Largo, or Largo* by itself, a middle movement: *Allegro,* and *Vivace,* a very brisk, swift, or fast movement: Piano, soft.

In his later *Sonatas in Four Parts* (probably written in the 1680s but not published until 1697), Purcell also used the Italian words *allegro, vivace, largo,* and *adagio.*[11] The marks *presto largo, poco largo,* and even *largo* alone, therefore denote in Purcell's sonatas a movement falling within the second category of tempo between fast and slow, as a movement of "middle" (meaning moderate) speed. In the concertos of Corelli and Handel, the marks *andante largo,* and *largo andante* may also be understood as indications of tempos between the faster and slower varieties and therefore relatively moderate in speed.

A comparison of three airs in triple meter from Purcell's *Dido and Aeneas* demonstrates how key, harmonic motion, and melody provide clues about the spirit, whether or not a tempo mark is present.[12] By itself, the meter 3/4 implies a moderate, or even quick, tempo as in "Come away, fellow sailors," where the key of F major and harmonic motion of one chord per measure support a lively tempo. For "Ah! Belinda," Purcell also employs 3/4 but the slower harmonic rhythm, more complex rhythmic motion in the melody, and the key of C minor suggest a slower pace, also confirmed by Purcell's mark, "slow." A third air, the famous lament "When I am laid in earth," has no tempo mark, but its meter (3/2) suggests an even slower pace than "Ah! Belinda" (in 3/4); the descending tetrachord and chromatic inflections in the bass line also contribute to a melancholic or pathetic affect.

The words *adagio* and *allegro* occur with some frequency in seventeenth-century instrumental music, but other musical features may give a clearer guide as to the appropriate tempo. A single sonata may have several short sections, each of which is marked *adagio* (or *largo*), with intervening sections marked *allegro,* but every one may require a different tempo. The character of each section and its speed are determined in large part by the predominant rhythms, the meter, and other musical characteristics.

In Buxtehude's Sonata for violin, viola da gamba, and harpsichord in A, Op. 2, No. 7 (Appendix A), sections are sometimes separated by a double bar and a new tempo mark, but most often by only a barline and change of meter. At a cadence in the improvisatory solo section for the violin, consisting of a fermata followed by two unaccompanied notes (m. 46), the violinist might elaborate the cadence as a transition to the next section. The best indications of character and tempo are the melodic and harmonic motion within each section. The opening section, for example, contains flowing triplet rhythms characteristic of the Italian *giga*. The ensuing section for solo violin with figuration over a static harmony should be played freely, in an improvisatory fashion. At the change of meter to 3/4 (m. 47), Buxtehude indicates *concitato*, literally "agitated" in character, with a regular pulse and sixteenth-note motion also used by Monteverdi in *concitato* passages. The harmonic motion of one chord per measure for this section permits a quick pace, still felt in three. At m. 120 a transitional section for solo viola da gamba may be taken somewhat freely, but less so than the violin's earlier improvisatory passage (m. 30), since the bass line has more rhythmic motion. An adagio (mm. 168–170) at the end of the allegro section denotes a halting of speed at the cadence. The final section over a quasi-ground bass begins at m. 171, without a tempo mark. The chromatic passing notes (mm. 173–177) in the violin suggest a fairly slow beginning for the 6/4, still felt in two, and a rapid, more virtuosic character at the poco presto.

The eighteenth-century adagio

As we have seen, the word *adagio* was used in numerous ways in the seventeenth century, but in general it indicates a contrast with what came before. Following an allegro, the word *adagio* literally means "at ease" or "not fast," but it does not necessarily imply a slow tempo.

In the eighteenth century the word *adagio* may imply more than merely a tempo. For example, Quantz distinguishes between two types of adagio according to the type of embellishment appropriate to each.[13] An adagio in the French style would incorporate ornaments primarily on individual notes, including various types of trills and vibrato; it would require "a clean and sustained execution of the air, and embellishment with the essential graces, such as appoggiaturas, whole- and half-shakes, mordents, turns, *battemens*, *flattemens*, etc., but no extensive passage work or significant addition of extempore embellishments." The Italian style, on the contrary requires "extensive artificial [that is, artful] graces that accord with the harmony . . . in addition to the little French embellishments." For performing Italian embellishment, he feels that the soloist needs a greater knowledge of harmony, so that diverse runs, appoggiaturas, leaps, and arpeggios can be improvised. Quantz's two categories of adagio fall into the melancholic (pathetic) type and a faster, cantabile type. It is important to distinguish between these two types, even though the tempo mark alone may not provide enough information to choose between them. One must be "in accordance with the prevailing sentiment, so that you do not play a very melancholy Adagio too quickly or a cantabile Adagio too slowly." He suggests several methods of making the distinction between the two types of adagio.[14]

First, a pathetic adagio may be identified by its meter since, as he observes, alla breve and 3/2 are generally beaten more slowly than C or 3/4. The pathetic adagio may also be distinguished by its key (see Table 2-1). He recommends that an adagio in G minor, A minor, C minor, F minor, or D♯ major be played "more mournfully and therefore more slowly than adagios in other keys." He cites the following tempo marks as appropriate for the two types:[15]

"Pathetic," slow adagio	"Cantabile" or somewhat faster adagio
Adagio di molto Lento assai	Cantabile Arioso Affettuoso Andante Andantino Largo Larghetto

In any of these adagio movements, according to Quantz, all notes are to be "caressed and flattered" with many small dynamic nuances, such as the *messa di voce* (a swell and diminuendo) on long notes, and with alternations of forte and piano.

At least three types of adagio are frequently encountered in the eighteenth century: (1) a middle movement marked *adagio*, often short, consisting usually of an imperfect half-cadence with some elaboration, either written out or implied, (2) *adagio* marked at the end of a movement to mean ritardando, or "slower than the prevailing tempo," and (3) a complete movement whose spirit must be determined from the meter, key, dissonance, and harmonic rhythm.

An adagio of the first type (a middle movement) merely links the surrounding fast movements and is therefore short. Adagios of this type can be found in Handel's *Solos for a German Flute, Hoboy, or Violin with a Thorough Bass for the Harpsichord* (Op. 1, 1724).[16] The third movement of Sonata No. 3 in A for violin and continuo, marked *adagio,* consists of a five-measure elaboration of a half-cadence in the relative minor (Example 2-1). It begins with a chord of F♯ minor and ends with a cadence on C♯, the dominant of F♯. The cadence is a Phrygian type, in which the bass resolves by half step while the upper part moves

Example 2-1. Handel, Sonata No. 3 in A for violin and continuo, third movement.

upward by whole step; the 7–6 suspension (or a similar appoggiatura) is typical of this type of adagio. In this case, Handel has written embellishments for the solo part, but in some other adagios from Op. 1, the embellishments must be added by the soloist. The two-note cadence marked adagio in Bach's Brandenburg Concerto No. 3 (BWV 1048) represents a middle "movement," but is so short that it retains only the typical imperfect half-cadence, in this case on the dominant of E minor (or V of vi in the original key).[17] The first violinist, as the leader of the ensemble, should add an embellishment using notes within the harmony to decorate the chords played by the strings.

An adagio of the second type is not a section or movement on its own, but merely a concluding cadence within a movement. Examples may be found in several of Handel's sonatas, including Sonata No. 3 in A for violin and continuo, where the first movement (andante) concludes with a half-cadence on E marked *adagio* (Example 2-2). In this context, adagio signifies a ritardando within the prevailing tempo, and it sometimes allows the soloist to add an embellishment at the cadence. Thus in Corelli's Sonata Op. 5, No. 5 for violin and continuo (Appendix A), an adagio at the end of the second movement (vivace) could be elaborated, as the mark *arpeggio* also suggests. Here the adagio forms both a concluding cadence for the vivace and a transition between movements. In the first movement (allegro) from Vivaldi's Concerto in D major for violin, strings, and continuo (RV 212a), a solo section for the violin concludes with a one-measure adagio at the cadence (m. 129), preceding the entry of the strings.[18] In this case too, adagio seems to allow the soloist the possibility of ornamenting the cadence. Or, the word *adagio* may imply simply a ritardando, as in an allegro from Vivaldi's Concerto RV 565 (Op. 3, No. 11). In a more unusual example, Bach's organ prelude "O Mensch, bewein' dein' Sünde gross" (BWV 622) from the *Orgel-Büchlein*, begins as an adagio assai, and the final cadence is marked *adagissimo*, also indicating a ritardando within the prevailing tempo, but here possibly also an expression of the words in the chorale ("long He hung on the cross").[19]

Example 2-2. Handel, Sonata No. 3 in A for violin and continuo, end of the first movement.

Other baroque tempo marks

Quantz classifies all tempos, both slow and fast, according to four general categories, which he relates in speed to the human pulse rate. Although these must be considered classifications made primarily for pedagogical purposes, his four categories nevertheless offer some useful observations about the relative speeds indicated by some eighteenth-century tempo marks. By comparing the four categories with Quantz's descriptions of bow stroke appropriate to each, we may gain some understanding of the resulting spirit of each type of movement (Table 2-2).

Table 2-2. Quantz's four categories of tempo and the way they are played.

(1) Allegro Allegro assai Allegro di molto Presto Vivace 1 pulse = half note	"a lively, very light, nicely detached, and very short bow stroke, especially in the accompaniment, where you must play more sportively than seriously in pieces of this kind; and yet a certain moderation of tone must also be observed."
(2) Allegretto Allegro ma non tanto Allegro non troppo Allegro non presto Allegro moderato 1 pulse = quarter note	"performed a little more seriously, with a rather heavy yet lively and suitably vigorous bow stroke. In the Allegretto the sixteenth notes in particular, like the eight notes in the Allegro, require a very short bow stroke, made with the wrist rather than the whole arm, and articulated rather than slurred. . . ."
(3) Arioso Cantabile Soave Dolce Poco andante Maestoso Pomposo Affettuoso Adagio spiritoso 1 pulse = eighth note	"executed quietly, and with a light bow stroke. Even if interspersed with quick notes of various kinds, the Arioso still requires a light and quiet stroke." "played seriously, with a rather heavy and sharp stroke."
(4) Adagio assai Pesante Lento Largo assai Mesto Grave 1 pulse = sixteenth note	"slow and melancholy . . . requires the greatest moderation of tone, and the longest, most tranquil, and heaviest [= most sustained] bow stroke."

From *Quantz*, 231.

The dances and their tempos

Certain movements, particularly when they form part of a suite, bear the titles of dances that provide a clue to their tempo. The meter, rhythm, phrasing, and character of each dance were implied by its title, and even when the dance is not identified, these same characteristics may help to determine the tempo of a piece. The flowing quality of the Italian *giga*, for example, can be felt in Bach's aria, "Doch weichet, ihr tollen," from *Liebster Gott, wenn werd ich sterben* (BWV 8; Appendix A), although it is not identified as a *giga*.

A list of the most common dances is shown in Table 2-3, with descriptions of their character and appropriate style of performance and comments from several baroque theorists. We should observe that some theorists' descriptions may differ about the character of certain dances. Of course, some dances that remained in vogue for a century or more gradually changed, their tempos becoming faster or slower as their character was modified. Thus, performers must take care to seek out descriptions of dances from the same geographical area and period as the music they wish to interpret. Not all movements that bear dance titles were intended to serve the function of accompaniment to actual dancing, but they usually preserve the character and mood associated with the dance.

Table 2-3. Baroque dances and their characteristics.

Sources:
> Freillon-Poncein, *La véritable manière de'apprendre à jouer en perfection du hautbois, de la flûte et du flageolet* (1700), 54–58.
> Brossard, *Dictionaire de musique* (1703).
> Mattheson, *Der volkommene Capellmeister* (1739), transl. Harriss, 453–468.
> Quantz, *On Playing the Flute* (1752), 291.
> Rousseau, *Dictionaire de musique* (1768).

Title of dance and description	France	Germany
allemande		
C or 4/4 moderately slow inequality usually on sixteenth notes	Brossard: "usually two beats per measure, sometimes four ... serious [*grave*]" Rousseau: "four beats per measure ... slow, but old-fashioned ... those who still play it give it a faster tempo."	Mattheson: "good order and calm ... the image of a content or satisfied spirit"
bourrée		
2 or ¢ similar to the rigaudon; inequality on eighth notes	Rousseau: "frequent syncopations ... lively [*gai*]"	Mattheson: "slow, calm, content, pleasant, agreeable" Quantz: played "gaily" with a "short and light bow stroke"

Table 2-3. Continued.

Title of dance and description	France	Germany
canary		
a type of gigue inequality on sixteenth notes	Rousseau: "faster than the gigue . . . not used any more"	Mattheson: "eager, swift . . . at the same time must sound with a little simplicity"
		Quantz: played with a "short, sharp" bow stroke
chaconne (see passacaille)		
3/4, begins on second beat	Freillon-Poncein: "beaten quickly in 3 or slowly in 1"	Mattheson: "usually major mode, often with a ground bass . . . more deliberate than the passacaille"
	Rousseau: "moderate speed, beats clearly marked, now used only in opera . . . formerly in either 2 or 3, but now in 3"	Quantz: played "majestically"
courante		
3/2 with hemiola begins with upbeat	Freillon-Poncein: "slow [fort lent]"	Mattheson: "hopeful"
	Rousseau: "serious [grave], not used any more"	Quantz: "played majestically . . . bow detached at each quarter note"
corrente		
3/4 or 3/8, Italian type, fast		
entrée		
duple meter		Mattheson: "noble and majestic; sharp and punctuated, not too pompous"
		Quantz: played "majestically . . . bow detached at each quarter note . . . slurs rarely used, quick notes detached"
forlana		
6/4 or 6/8 from Venice; inquality in eighth notes; rhythm similar to loure	Brossard: "dotted rhythms"	
	Rousseau: "quick [gai]"	
gavotte		
₵ or 2, begins with upbeat	Freillon-Poncein: "very slow [fort lentement] . . . like the bourée but more serious [fort lentement] . . . with more touching expression"	Mattheson: "true jubilation, with a skipping nature, not running"

Table 2-3. Continued.

Title of dance and description	France	Germany
[gavotte]	Brossard: "sometimes quick [*gai*], sometimes slow [*grave*]" Rousseau: "gracious [*gracieux*], often quick [*gai*], sometimes tender and slow"	
gigue 6/8 or 6/4 English origin similar to loure but faster	Freillon-Poncein: "slow duple meter [*grave*]"	Mattheson: "ardent fleeting zeal" Quantz: played with a "short and light bow stroke"
giga 9/8 or 12/8	Rousseau: "fairly quick [*assez gai*] ... not used any more in Italy, and hardly in France either"	Mattheson: "extreme speed, volatility ... frequently in a flowing, uninterrupted manner"
loure a type of gigue 6/4 or 6/8 begins with upbeat	Rousseau: "rather slow [*assez lent*] ... one dots the first note and makes the second one short ... loure is an old instrument similar to the musette on which the dance was played"	"Mattheson: "proud and arrogant" Quantz: played majestically ... bow detached at each quarter note"
menuet 3/4	Rousseau: "formerly very quick and fast [*fort gaie, fort vîte*], but now with an elegant and noble simplicity, more moderate"	Mattheson: "moderate cheerfulness" Quantz: played "springily ... quarter notes are marked with a rather heavy, but still short bow stroke"
musette 3/4 or 3/8	Rousseau: "two or three beats per measure, long notes in the bass"	
passacaille 3/4 similar to chaconne	Freillon-Poncein and Brossard: "more tender than a chaconne, almost always minor" Rousseau: "a type of chaconne but slower, more tender"	Mattheson and Quantz: "like the chaconne, but a little faster"

Table 2-3. Continued.

Title of dance and description	France	Germany
passepied 3/8 with hemiola begins with upbeat	Freillon-Poncein: "a little faster than menuet" Rousseau: "felt in 1 . . . simmilar to menuet, except for syncopations . . . faster"	Mattheson: "pleasant frivolity" Quantz: "lighter and slightly faster than the menuet"
rigaudon ¢, 2, or 2/4 begins with upbeat	Freillon-Poncein: "similar to bourée" Rousseau: "quick [gai]"	Mattheson: "character of a trifling joke" Quantz: played "gaily" with a "short and light bow stroke"
rondeau		Quantz: "played rather tranquillly"
sarabande eighth notes unequal	Freillon-Poncein: "slow [lent]" Rousseau: serious [grave]; "formerly danced with castanets . . . not used any more"	Mattheson: "serious, expresses ambition" Quantz: "majestic . . . with a more agreeable execution than the entrée or loure"
tambourin 2 or 2/4 Provençal origin bass restrikes same note, imitating the tambourin usually begins on the second beat	Rousseau: "much in style . . . very quick [très gai], jumpy, well-cadenced"	Quantz: "a little faster than the bourée or gigue, otherwise played like it"

Bibliographical notes

For further reading about the tactus, various meters, and their relationship to tempo, see the articles "Notation (III)," "Stile Concitato," and "Tempo and Expression Marks" in *Grove*. In the same dictionary, the articles "Affections, Doctrine of the," "Figures, Doctrine of Musical," and "Rhetoric and Music" are also helpful.

George Houle presents theoretical evidence on the origin and meaning of time signatures. David Lasocki provides an informative explanation of the passions as viewed by Quantz, Mattheson, and others. For the relationship of affect and dance, see especially Gregory Butler's "The Projection of Affect in Baroque

Dance Music," in which the author discusses the relationship of dynamics, articulation, and phrasing to affect in the writings of Mace and Mattheson. Related
studies are those of Patricia Ranum and Wendy Hilton. Hilton includes a description of the steps, phrasing, rhythmic patterns, and ornamentation in the courante
from treatises published between 1623 and 1725.

FOR FURTHER STUDY

Aldrich, Putnam. *Rhythm in Seventeenth-Century Italian Monody: with an Anthology of Songs and Dances.* London: Dent, 1966.

Barnett, Dene. *The Art of Gesture: the Practices and Principles of 18th-Century Acting.* Hamburg: Carl Winter, 1987.

Barnett, Dene, and Ian Parker. "Finding the Appropriate Attitude." *EM* 8 no. 1 (January 1980): 65–69.

Buelow, George J. "Music, Rhetoric, and the Concept of the Affections: a Selective Bibliography." *Notes* 30 no. 2 (1973–1974): 250–259.

Butler, Gregory. "The Projection of Affect in Baroque Dance Music." *EM* 12 no. 2 (May 1984): 201–207.

_____ . "Music and Rhetoric in Early Seventeenth-Century English Sources." *MQ* 66 no. 1 (1980): 53–64.

Cudworth, Charles. "The Meaning of 'Vivace' in Eighteenth Century England." *Fontes artis musicae* 12 (1965): 194–195.

Donington, Robert. *Tempo and Rhythm in Bach's Organ Music.* New York: Hinrichsen Edition, 1960.

Haynes, Bruce. "Tonality and the Baroque Oboe." *EM* 7 no. 3 (July 1979): 355–357.

Hilton, Wendy. "A Dance for Kings: the Seventeenth-Century French Courante." *EM* 5 no. 2 (April 1977): 161–172.

Houle, George. *Meter in Music, 1600–1800: Performance, Perception, Notation.* Bloomington: Indiana University Press, 1987.

Lasocki, David. "Quantz and the Passions: Theory and Practice." *EM* 6 (October 1978): 556–565.

Little, Meredith Ellis. "The Contribution of Dance Steps to Musical Analysis and Performance: La Bourgogne." *JAMS* 28 no. 1 (Spring, 1975): 112–124.

Marshall, Robert. "Tempo and Dynamic Indications in the Bach Sources: a Review of the Terminology." In *Bach, Handel, and Scarlatti: Tercentenary Essays,* ed. Peter Williams, 259–275. Cambridge: Cambridge University Press, 1985.

Mather, Betty Bang, with Dean M. Karns. *Dance Rhythms in the French Baroque: a Handbook for Performance.* Bloomington: Indiana University Press, 1988.

Mendel, Arthur. Preface to J. S. Bach's *The Passion According to St. John.* New York: Schirmer, 1951.

_____ . "A Brief Note on Triple Proportion in Schütz." *MQ* 46 (January 1960): 67–70.

_____ . "Some Ambiguities of the Mensural System," *Studies in Music History: Essays for Oliver Strunk.* Ed. Harold Powers, 137–160. Princeton: Princeton University Press, 1968.

Neumann, Frederick. "The Use of Baroque Treatises on Musical Performance." *ML* 48 (1967): 315–324.

Powell, Newman W. "The Function of the Tactus in the Performance of Renaissance Music." *The Musical Heritage of the Church* 6 (1963): 64–84.

_____ . "Kirnberger on Dance Rhythms, Fugues, and Characterization." In *Festschrift Theodore Hoelty-Nickel.* Ed. N. W. Powell, 66–76. Valparaiso, Indiana: Valparaiso University, 1967.

Ranum, Patricia. "Audible Rhetoric and Mute Rhetoric: the Seventeenth-Century French Sarabande." *EM* 14 no. 1 (February 1986): 22–39.

Ruff, Lillian M. "M.-A. Charpentier's 'Règles de composition'." *The Consort* 24 (1967): 233–270.

Sachs, Curt. *Rhythm and Tempo: a Study in Music History*. New York: Norton, 1953.

Schwandt, Erich. "L'Affilard on the French Court Dances." *MQ* 60 (1974): 389–400.

NOTES TO CHAPTER 2

1. Thomas Mace, *Musick's Monument* (London, 1676; R New York, Broude Brothers, 1966), 80–81.
2. *MonteverdiW*, v. 8:1, 107 and 88.
3. *MonteverdiW* v. 8:1, foreword (n.p.). For an English translation, see *Strunk*, 413–415.
4. Mattheson, *Der volkommene Capellmeister*, transl. Harriss, 432.
5. Charles de Brosses, *Lettres d'Italie du Président de Brosses*, ed. Frédéric d'Agay (Paris: Mercure de France, 1986), 2: 300–303.
6. A tempo mark of *allegro* was added to the aria in the Walsh edition published the same year as the first performance (*Flavius an Opera . . . Publish'd by the Author*); see Winton Dean and John Merrill Knapp, *Handel's Opera, 1704–1726* (Oxford: Clarendon Press, 1987), 481.
7. *Musica religiosa* (1610), *MonteverdiW*, v. 14:2, 310, 294, 287.
8. *SchützW*, v. 16 ed. Werner Bittinger (Kassel: Bärenreiter, 1965), 20, 12.
9. *PurcellW*, v. 31 ed. Thurston Dart (1959).
10. *PurcellW*, v. 5 ed. Michael Tilmouth, p. x; the preface is also in *Rowen*, 176–178.
11. *PurcellW*, v. 5.
12. Henry Purcell, *Dido and Aeneas*, ed. Curtis Price, Norton Critical Scores (New York: Norton, 1986), 90, 153, 176.
13. *Quantz*, 162–163.
14. *Quantz*, 162–178.
15. *Quantz*, 164–165.
16. G. F. Handel, *The Complete Sonatas for Treble (Alto) Recorder and Basso Continuo*, ed. David Lasocki and Walter Bergmann (London: Faber, 1979); *The Complete Sonatas for Flute and Basso Continuo*, ed. David Lasocki (London: Faber, 1983); *The Complete Sonatas for Violin and Basso Continuo*, ed. Terence Best (London: Faber, 1983).
17. On the frequent use of the Phrygian cadence as a middle movement in the seventeenth and eighteenth centuries, see Jan LaRue, "Bifocal Tonality: an Explanation for Ambiguous Baroque Cadences," in *Essays in Honor of Archibald T. Davison by His Associates* (Cambridge: Harvard University, Department of Music, 1957), 173–184.
18. *VivaldiW*, v. 312, 18.
19. Johann Sebastian Bach, *Orgelbüchlein*, facs. ed. Heinz-Harald Löhlein, Documenta musicologica 2:11 (Kassel: Bärenreiter, 1981) 29. Also in *NBA*, series 4:1, 40–41.

3

Dynamics

The use of different dynamics in music forms part of its expression, and for the baroque musician dynamic nuance added significantly to music's ability to arouse the "passions" in its listeners. Within phrases and even on single notes, dynamic nuances were used liberally by singers and instrumentalists, though they were rarely indicated in the score.

The sparseness of dynamic marks in baroque music gave twentieth-century interpreters the mistaken notion that dynamic contrasts occurred primarily in large blocks that were either loud or soft, a principle called terrace dynamics. This notion was supported by the infrequent appearance of crescendo or decrescendo marks in baroque scores and the natural tutti-solo contrast found in many baroque concertos. The harpsichord and organ also inherently produce dynamic terraces by the use of different registrations. David Boyden challenged the notion of terrace dynamics as the principal type of gradation by investigating both theoretical and musical sources of the seventeenth and eighteenth centuries. He demonstrated that subtle dynamic shadings were very much a feature of baroque performance in addition to echoes and other *forte* and *piano* contrasts.

Written and unwritten dynamic nuances in the seventeenth century

One of the earliest descriptions of expressive dynamic nuance is found in Caccini's *Le Nuove Musiche* (1602). In a detailed preface to his airs, he describes the nuances associated with the new style of singing, such as the *esclamatione*, "a strengthening [*crescendo*] of the voice"[1] (i.e., a swell). Since the *esclamatione*, in Caccini's view, sometimes sounded harsh, particularly in falsetto, he recommends the use of a diminuendo on a long note, to give it "a bit more spirit [*un poco più spirto*]" and make it "more affective [*per muovere l'affetto*]." These two dynamic nuances are applied as ornaments to enhance the expression of the words, and for Caccini they form the foundation of singing in a "passionate" manner. He recommends, however, that these effects should not be used in cheerful and lively airs.

Caccini's ideas were taken up by followers of the new style in Rome and also in England, especially in the works of Claudio Monteverdi, Girolamo Fantini, and Dario Castello (fl. 1621–1644). The expressive swell and the diminuendo on a single note belong to both vocal and instrumental performance from the early seventeenth century onward. Echo effects are marked frequently in early seventeenth-century instrumental music as well, as Fantini's sonata for two trumpets demonstrates (Example 3-1). In Dario Castello's Sonata No. 9 *Sonate concertate* (Bk. I, 1621), a *forte* passage is first played by the bassoon and then imitated *piano* by violin I and *più piano* by violin II (Example 3-2).

Despite evidence of successive dynamic marks to imply a crescendo or diminuendo in music by Domenico Mazzocchi (1638), Leonhard Lechler (ca. 1640), and Matthew Locke (1672),[2] it is rare to find more than a *forte* or *piano* marking in scores and parts of the seventeenth century. Alessandro Stradella's instrumental music is full of textural contrast between a tutti (ripieno) group and a solo group, but this dynamic contrast is inherent in the writing. In the *Sonata a*

Example 3-1. Girolamo Fantini, Sonata for two unaccompanied trumpets, from *Modo per Imparare a sonare di tromba* (1638).

Example 3-2. Dario Castello, Sonata No. 9 from *Sonate concertate*, Book 1 (1621).

otto viole con una tromba[3] he divides the eight viols (probably played on four different sizes of instrument) into two choirs, and a few *piano* marks in the second *coro* set off short echo passages.

Corelli's *Sonate da chiesa* (Op. 1, 1681; Op. 3, 1689) for two violins and continuo uses *forte* and *piano* contrast to a greater extent, most often in one of three ways: (1) as an echo effect within one part (last allegro of Op. 3, Sonata No. 3), (2) as an echo marked *piano* for both violins simultaneously (last allegro of Op. 3, Sonata No. 2), and (3) for the concluding phrase of a section, where *piano* appears in all three parts (vivace of Op. 3, Sonata No. 1).[4]

The use of *piano* to end a section is also found in both slow and fast movements in Corelli's *Sonate da camera* for two violins and continuo (Op. 2, 1685; Op. 4, 1694) and the *Concerti grossi*, Op. 6 (1714).[5] The latter collection contains more dynamic marks than do the trios; although rarely more than *f* or *p*, Corelli does employ them in a variety of ways within the solo and tutti groups. A favorite technique is to mark the end of a section *piano*, as in the *giga* (last movement) of Sonata Op. 5, No. 5 (Appendix A), or in the second allegro of Concerto No. 7 (Op. 6), where the melody drops an octave at the beginning of the *piano*. The successive chords marked *p–f–p–f* at the beginning of No. 7 show an effective use of extremes in dynamic contrast.[6] In the "Christmas" Concerto (No. 8) the *f–p–pp* marking implies a diminuendo at the end of the pastorale.[7] Using these and other similar marks as a guide, one may add both graded dynamics (for entire phrases) and nuanced ones (on single notes) in other Italian instrumental music of the seventeenth century, even when not specifically indicated.

In Buxtehude's Sonatas for violin, viola da gamba, and harpsichord (Op. 1 and 2, 1694 and 1696), only a few dynamic marks are found in the printed parts. Most frequently one finds a *piano* within an allegro section to show an echo effect. Buxtehude rarely employs Corelli's technique of ending a section with a *piano* phrase, although this does occur in Sonata No. 6 from Op. 1.[8]

Written and implied dynamics in eighteenth-century music

The use of crescendo or diminuendo (——⊏ or ⊐——) is more extensive in the eighteenth century, beginning with Giovanni Antonio Piani's sonatas for violin and continuo (Op. 1, Paris 1712).[9] Rameau also used the signs ——⊏ and ⊐—— in a printed score of *Hippolyte et Aricie* (1733) for an unusually dramatic effect. In act I, when Phèdre unleashes her fury against the lovers Hippolyte and Aricie, the printed score shows some crescendo and diminuendo marks during the orchestral "thunder" [*tonnerre*], as well as some sudden changes to *forte* after a diminuendo (see Figure 1). Eyewitness accounts of eighteenth-century performances also mention the effect of an orchestral crescendo or diminuendo, or the contrast of a sudden *forte*.

The swell and diminuendo on a single note (or *messa di voce*) continued to be regarded as an expressive ornament which could be applied on a long note, but it was rarely indicated in the music. Many treatises introduce the swell and diminuendo as an important concept to be learned almost as soon as one can produce a long tone. Certain other ornaments also carried an implied dynamic shading, such as the appoggiatura, whose dissonance was louder than its resolution. Quantz provides an ornamented adagio as an example of a slow movement with nuances, including crescendo and diminuendo as well as strong and weak stresses added with the tongue or bow stroke.[10] His adagio is ornamented with trills, passing notes, and other melodic figures, with a different nuance on almost every note, added according to the metrical stress, melodic direction, and phrasing.

Although Italian dynamic indications were used in most places throughout Europe, in France one finds either French or Italian designations, sometimes even in the same piece. In French scores, *f* corresponds to the French term *fort* (loud), *ff* to *très fort* (very loud), *p* to *doux* (soft), *pp* to *très doux* (very soft), and *à demi jeu* represents a midpoint between *f* and *p*. Given the absence of such marks as *mf* and *mp* and the relatively rare occurrence of crescendo and diminuendo in baroque scores, it seems likely that composers sometimes implied a diminuendo with *f–p–pp*. Modern performers should consider the musical context carefully when interpreting marks, for a sudden change of level may be inappropriate.

One additional convention of notation should be mentioned in relation to dynamics, namely the use of *piano* as a cue to the instrumental players when the

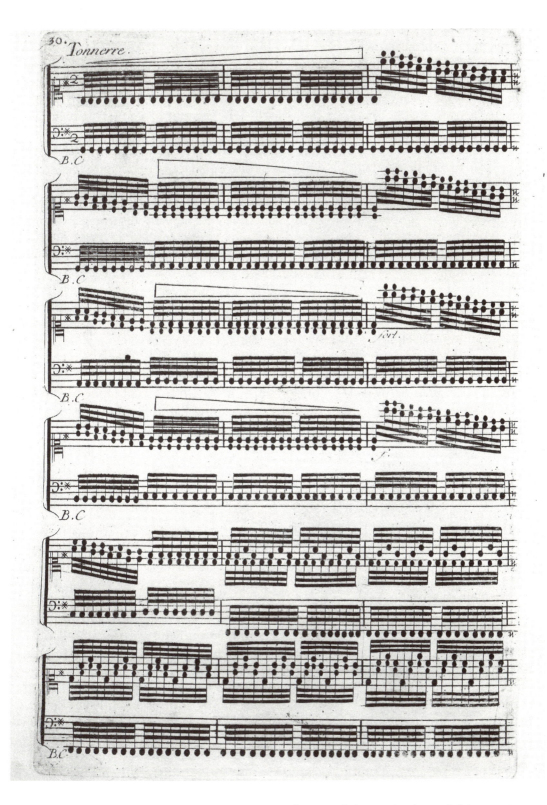

Figure 1. Jean-Philippe Rameau, *Tonnerre* [thunder], from *Hippolyte et Aricie*, act I, scene 4 (Paris, 1733), with crescendo and diminuendo marks.

voice enters in an aria or other solo piece. When the singer's phrase is finished, a *forte* in the instrumental parts will show that the instruments play alone. These marks were intended merely as a guide to instrumentalists in their role as accompanists and should not be taken literally as terraced levels of sound. This use of *piano* and *forte* can be found in many of Bach's cantatas in arias that have one or more obbligato instruments. In the aria "Doch weichet, ihr tollen," from J. S. Bach's *Liebster Gott, wenn werd ich sterben* (BWV 8), dynamic marks of this sort are found in the flute and string parts (Appendix A, mm. 16, 18, and 20, for example).

The mark *pp*, according to Walther, meant *più piano* or softer, but not necessarily *pianissimo*. Bach sometimes used the mark *pp* in this sense, but it is often difficult for modern players to tell what mark Bach used originally, since modern editors frequently (though incorrectly) expand Bach's *pp* into *pianissimo*.

Dynamic marks are rarely found in Bach's orchestral suites (ouvertures), but he uses them more liberally in the Brandenburg Concertos, a copy of which he dedicated in 1721 to Christian Ludwig, Margrave of Brandenburg. In the first movement of Concerto No. 3 (BWV 1048) for three violins, three violas, three cellos, and continuo (with violone), Bach uses *piano* and *forte* within groups of instruments to set off thematically important material exchanged between instruments, and to highlight harmonic arrivals at important structural points.[11] A similar treatment of dynamics can be seen in Concerto No. 2 (BWV 1047) and, somewhat less frequently marked, in Handel's Concerti Grossi Op. 6 (*Twelve Grand Concertos in Seven Parts*, London, 1740).[12] In other eighteenth-century instrumental music such as the concertos of Bach and Handel, dynamics may be added according to the principles observed in the Brandenburg concertos.

The relationship of dynamics to harmony

Quantz advises the continuo players, both harpsichordist and cellist, to consider the amount of dissonance and consonance between the solo and continuo part when adding dynamic nuance. He directs that "to excite the different passions the dissonances must be struck more strongly than the consonances" (Quantz, 254). He explains that these effects can be accomplished by varying the texture of the right-hand part and by the speed of arpeggiation; thus, a thick chord arpeggiated quickly will sound *forte*, and a thinner chord arpeggiated more slowly will sound softer. An instrument with two keyboards has the additional possibility of using the upper keyboard (with one eight-foot register) to accompany soft sections and the lower (with two eight-foot registers plucking simultaneously) to accompany *forte* passages. As Quantz indicates, both keyboards may be used by the player along with a variety of arpeggiations and textures in continuo playing:

> On a harpsichord with one keyboard, passages marked Piano may be produced by a moderate touch and by diminishing the number of parts, those marked Mezzo Forte by doubling the bass in octaves, those marked Forte in the same manner and also by taking some *con-*

sonances belonging to the chord into the left hand, and those marked Fortissimo by quick arpeggiations of the chords from below upwards, by the same doubling of the octaves and the consonances in the left hand, and by a more vehement and forceful touch. On a harpsichord with two keyboards, you have the additional advantage of being able to use the upper keyboard for the Pianissimo (Quantz, 259).

He illustrates the foregoing principles with a movement (Example 3-3) in which he marks the appropriate dynamics for the accompaniment. This manner of accompanying attempts "an imitation of the human voice, and of such instruments as are capable of swelling and diminishing the tone" (Quantz, 256). He

Example 3-3. Quantz, An adagio with dynamic marks to illustrate the manner of accompanying a solo.

recommends accompanying the consonant chords of an adagio "not with the greatest possible force, but generally Mezzo Piano, so that you retain the ability to play more softly or loudly wherever it is necessary." Quantz also categorizes different types of dissonances between the melody and bass according to the strength of sound they require. Among the strongest are the diminished seventh (mm. 15, 31) and the augmented fourth (m. 24). The dynamic levels of *p–mf–f–ff* are indicated in the continuo part to show how the accompanist should consider the dissonance and consonance between the melody and bass and adjust the texture and sound accordingly. The cellist or other sustaining bass instrument would also reinforce these dynamic nuances by paying close attention to the harmonic language. It is worth noting that Quantz's marks incorporate a metrical stress on most, but not all, downbeats. The bass line derives its dynamic shading from the harmony and accentuation of the melody, creating a subtle shading even on passages of repeated eighth notes.

In considering the various possibilities for using dynamics in baroque music, the modern performer must first determine whether written marks originate with the composer, and if so, what their meaning may have been. When dynamics are enclosed within parentheses or brackets in a modern edition, they are usually the editor's suggestion and need be incorporated only if they suit the tempo, spirit, instrumentation, and other features of a particular performance. In most baroque music, long crescendos and diminuendos are special effects. When not marked, they may best be reserved for a pictorial context (such as a storm in an opera) or for dramatic purposes, as in a unison passage performed by the tutti group of a concerto. More common—indeed essential—are the dynamic nuances performed within phrases and on single notes, which may be combined with occasional use of vibrato and with certain types of ornaments (to be discussed in chapter 8). These nuances belong to the shaping of baroque harmony and melody, and even when they are absent from the written score, an effective performance relies to a considerable extent upon their introduction.

Bibliographical notes

David Boyden demonstrated convincingly that terrace dynamics were not the only, or even the principal, type of gradation used in baroque music; he cites significant theoretical and musical evidence supporting the use of both graded and nuanced dynamics. Quantz's example of a melodic line with dynamic nuances is transcribed into a modern score by Hans-Peter Schmitz, and by Betty Bang Mather and David Lasocki in the volumes listed below. Robert Marshall provides new observations about marks used by Bach at different periods of his life. On the use of dynamic marks in Vivaldi's music (and for other matters related to performance), see Walter Kolneder's informative study.

FOR FURTHER STUDY

Boyden, David. "Dynamics in Seventeenth- and Eighteenth-Century Music." In *Essays in Honor of Archibald T. Davison by His Associates*, 185–193. Cambridge: Harvard University, Department of Music, 1957.

Harding, Rosamond E. M. "On the Origins and History of the Forte and Piano, the Crescendo and Diminuendo." In *Origins of Musical Time and Expression*, 85–107. London: Oxford University Press, 1938.

Hering, Hans. "Die Dynamik in Joh. Seb. Bachs Klaviermusik." *BJ* 38 (1949–50): 65–80.

Kolneder, Walter. *Aufführungspraxis bei Vivaldi* (Leipzig: Breitkopf & Härtel, 1955). Transl. Anne de Dadelsen as *Performance Practices in Vivaldi* (Winterthur, Switzerland: Amadeus Verlag, 1979).

Marshall, Robert L. "Tempo and Dynamic Indications in the Bach Sources: a Review of the Terminology." In *Bach, Handel, Scarlatti: Tercentenary Essays*, ed. Peter F. Williams, 259–275. Cambridge: Cambridge University Press, 1985. Also published as "Tempo and Dynamics: the Original Terminology," in *The Music of Johann Sebastian Bach: the Sources, the Style, the Significance* (New York: Schirmer Books, 1989), 255–269.

Mather, Betty Bang, and David Lasocki. *Free Ornamentation in Woodwind Music, 1700–1775*. New York: McGinnis & Marx, 1976.

Robison, J. O. "The Messa di Voce as an Instrumental Ornament in the Seventeenth and Eighteenth Centuries." *MR* 43 no. 1 (1982): 1–14.

Schmitz, Hans-Peter. *Prinzipien der Aufführungspraxis alter Musik*. Berlin: Knauer-Verlag, 1950.

[Symposium] "Dynamik und Agogik in der Musik des Barock." In *Bericht über den siebenten internationalen Musikwissenschaftlichen Kongress Köln 1958*, 343–349. Kassel: Bärenreiter, 1959.

NOTES TO CHAPTER 3

1. Giulio Caccini, *Le nuove musiche* (1602), *ai lettori*, n.p.

2. Specific musical and theoretical evidence is cited by David Boyden, "Dynamics in Seventeenth- and Eighteenth-Century Music," *Essays in Honor of Archibald T. Davison by His Associates* (Cambridge: Harvard University, Department of Music, 1957), 186–188.

3. A. Stradella, *Sonata a otto viole con una tromba*, ed. Edward H. Tarr (Paris: Éditions Costallat, 1968).

4. *CorelliW*, v. 2 (*Sonate da camera, opus II und IV*), ed. Jürg Stenzl (Laaber: Laaber-Verlag, 1986), and v. 4 (*Concerti grossi, opus VI*), ed. Rudolf Bossard (Cologne: Arno Volk Verlag-Hans Gerig, 1978).

5. *CorelliW*, v. 1 (*Sonate da chiesa, opus I und III*), ed. Max Lütolf (Laaber: Laaber-Verlag, 1987), pp. 39f, 129, 119.

6. *CorelliW*, v. 4, 159.

7. Ibid., 190.

8. *DDT*, v. 11.

9. G. A. Piani, *Sonatas for Violin Solo and Violoncello with Cembalo*, ed. Barbara Garvey Jackson, Recent Researches in the Music of the Baroque Era, v. 20 (Madison: A-R Editions, 1975).

10. *Quantz*, 169–172. The piece is transcribed into modern notation in Betty Bang Mather and David Lasocki, *Free Ornamentation in Woodwind Music*, 68–74.

11. J. S. Bach, *NBA*, ser. 7:2, v. 3, ed. Heinrich Besseler (Kassel: Bärenreiter, 1956), 64, 84.

12. *HandelW*, ser. 4, v. 14, ed. Adolf Hoffmann and Hans Ferdinand Redlich (Kassel: Bärenreiter, 1961).

4

Pitch, Tuning, and Temperament

Before the twentieth century, pitch levels for musical performance varied from place to place by as much as a third or more. Because practices were so variable, it is often impossible to document them precisely. Several baroque and later theorists attempted to measure frequencies, but not until J. H. Scheibler's *Tonmesser* in 1834 were these attempts accurate enough to be reliable. The first declaration of a standard pitch was made in France in 1859, when a^1 at 435 Hz (vibrations per second) was adopted by ministerial decree. The same standard was also adopted by several other countries, but international agreement was not reached until 1939, when $a^1 = 440$ Hz became the new standard. Today, many symphony orchestras exceed this pitch, and some performers (especially singers) have expressed a desire to halt the upward trend by formal agreement.

Interest in documenting the history of pitch began in the mid-nineteenth century, and in 1880 A. J. Ellis undertook a comprehensive attempt to collect and tabulate hundreds of pitch standards in use from Praetorius's time onward. Subsequent analyses of Ellis's findings, together with new documents and measurements of wind instruments and organs, have added much to our knowledge of early pitches, although interpretation of the evidence is by no means complete. Arthur Mendel also reevaluated the existing evidence and added significantly to it. Nevertheless, there are some ambiguities in the sources that have sparked disagreements among scholars, and further studies will undoubtedly be needed to address these issues.

The nonstandard nature of baroque pitches and temperaments

In the baroque era, both pitch and the relative tuning system, or temperament, varied considerably. Even within a given city, church organs were tuned to different pitches, and music for the opera or other secular uses was performed at different pitches too. Players either owned several instruments or adapted their instrument with crooks, extra joints, or different strings in order to perform in various surroundings. Given the variety of pitches that were used and the difficulty of documenting practices of the baroque era, it is not surprising that certain problems of interpretation remain. Most of our information comes from the pitch levels of surviving instruments and from early written documents that describe the most common pitch levels in use.

Of the instruments used during the seventeenth and eighteenth centuries, the strings and harpsichord were capable of the greatest variation in pitch. Depending upon the strength and thickness of their strings, they were capable of being tuned to pitches within the range of at least a half step, or even a whole step, in order to accord with other less flexible instruments. John Playford (1623–1686?) directs viol players to tune the top string as high as it "conveniently will bear" without breaking, and then to tune the others to it.[1] Horns and flutes were often equipped with extra crooks or joints which changed the instrument's pitch level so that it could more easily match the pitch and temperament of other instruments in a group. Quantz describes a flute with six middle joints or *corps de rechange* (added after about 1720), which allowed the instrument to vary its pitch level within an interval of almost a minor third.[2] Recorders, sackbuts, and oboes were usually constructed for playing at a given pitch level, for example that of the church organ. The reed of an oboe or bassoon, however, was adjustable to an extent to allow for variations of pitch caused by the temperature of the room or the instrument as it was being played. On a two-manual harpsichord, one keyboard sometimes plucked a set of strings a fourth or a fifth apart from that of the other keyboard, thus permitting the player to transpose a piece with ease.

Quantz observed that "the pitch regularly used for tuning in an orchestra has always varied considerably according to time and place."[3] This diversity he felt to be "most detrimental to music," because singers who perform arias in places where a high pitch level is used can scarcely perform the same pieces if they visit other localities where a low pitch is used. For singers and players of strings, brass, and woodwinds, playing in different temperaments demanded adjustments either on the instrument itself or in the player's technique. Quantz advocated the use of a single pitch standard, but his wish was not realized until two centuries later.

There is no international standard today for the temperament used in performance, but equal temperament is preferred for modern keyboard instruments. In this system, all the semitones within an octave are equally spaced from each other. All fifths are slightly flatter than perfect, and major thirds are fairly wide. Since the semitones are equally spaced, all intervals of the same type sound the same. Even though thirds, fourths, and fifths are all somewhat out of tune, many of us have become accustomed to equal temperament and scarcely notice its disadvantages. Music with chromatic passages or enharmonic notes (such as E♯ and F) is especially well-suited to equal temperament, but in some situations another choice may be better. Choirs and chamber ensembles often adapt the temperament by inflecting (raising or lowering) certain pitches to make some chords sound more in tune than they are in equal temperament, or to increase their "pull" in a harmonic context.

Equal temperament was described centuries ago by theorists, but it did not come into general use until the nineteenth century. In the baroque era, there were dozens of different temperaments in use, each one favoring certain keys since it had some intervals that were more in tune, or pure sounding, than they are in equal temperament. These temperaments restricted the number of keys in which an instrument could play, and composers therefore rarely used keys with more than three sharps or flats. Since most baroque music was not composed for equal temperament, performing a piece in an appropriate historical temperament will often bring out aspects of its dissonance treatment that would otherwise be hidden. When Louis Couperin's Prelude in F for harpsichord (Appendix A) is performed in meantone temperament, one of the most common of seventeenth-century temperaments, the contrast is heightened between the consonant, restful sound of F major and other chords with sevenths or passing dissonances. The listener's ear is aware of the different sizes of certain intervals, especially the adjacent half steps. Meantone temperament even helps the player to interpret the unmeasured notation (see chapter 7), since one may choose to linger over certain dissonances to increase their tension and pass quickly through others in order to dwell on the resolution. Unequal temperaments also add interest to a musical sequence, for example, since each time a motive is stated, it sounds slightly different. In Handel's aria, "Sirti, scogli, tempeste," from *Flavio* (Appendix A), the statement and repetition of a melodic fragment at different pitches in mm. 22 and 23 sound novel, because the semitones in the chromatic figures are not quite the same size. Thus, the temperament contributes to the music's affect and becomes one of many expressive means at the performer's disposal.

Northern Germany: The background to Bach's pitches

In northern Germany during Bach's lifetime, two pitch levels were in common use: *Chor-Ton* (also called *Zinck-Ton* or *Cornet-Ton*) or "choir pitch," and *Cammer-Ton* or "chamber pitch." The relationship between them was expressed by most writers in relative terms: *Cammer-Ton* was lower than *Chor-Ton* by a whole step, and in some places by a minor third. Organs were usually built at the higher *Chor-Ton*, thus allowing the pipes to be shorter and therefore less costly. Brass instruments usually played at the organ's pitch. Woodwind and string instruments most often tuned to *Cammer-Ton*. Thus when a group of instruments played with the organ, as in a cantata, some players either transposed at sight, or their parts were prepared to accommodate the two different pitches.

In order to describe the interval of difference between the two pitches, the theorist Jacob Adlung (1768) ascribed two names to the *Cammer-Ton* pitches in use.[4] He reports that in some regions *Chor-Ton* and *Cammer-Ton* were a tone apart; this chamber pitch he called *hoher* (higher) *Cammer-Ton* and placed it a tone below *Chor-Ton*. When the two pitches were a minor third apart, he called the chamber pitch *tiefer* (lower) *Cammer-Ton*. Although *Chor-Ton* was by no means set at a given frequency, this evidence suggests that it was relatively standard, and other theoretical evidence suggests that in northern Germany it had been so since the early seventeenth century.

Praetorius, who uses the same terms in his *De organographia* of 1619, provided meticulously detailed illustrations of the measurements for organ pipes and their pitches,[5] but his information has received different interpretations from modern scholars. Mendel concludes that *Chor-Ton* was at approximately a^1, 490 (or about our b^1),[6] whereas Myers and Haynes put it at 460 (approximately b^1 flat).[7] Cary Karp considered such factors as the possible shrinkage or expansion of the paper on which Praetorius's scale drawings of organ pipes were printed, and argues for *Chor-Ton* between a^1, 445 and a^1, 460. He also cites surviving instruments of the type Praetorius illustrates which are pitched near a^1, 450.[8] Given the fact that most eighteenth-century pitches were *lower* than *Chor-Ton*, the weight of evidence—including the pitches of extant north-German organs—favors a *Chor-Ton* pitched in the upper end of the range between 445 and 460.

Whatever Praetorius's absolute pitch was, it was used in the early seventeenth century for both *Chor-Ton* and *Cammer-Ton*. This pitch level survived in the eighteenth century for the sacred music of Johann Kuhnau (1660–1722) and Bach, and it also became known as "old *Chor-Ton*."

Haynes notes that *Cammer-Ton* was introduced in the 1680s with the arrival from France of newly invented woodwind instruments such as the flute and oboe.[9] As late as 1752, Quantz describes that "unpleasant choir pitch had prevailed for some centuries in Germany." Kuhnau reports in 1717 that when he became director at the Thomaskirche in 1702, he almost immediately eliminated the use of "cornet pitch" (*Chor-Ton*) and substituted *Cammer-Ton*, "which is a second or a minor third lower," depending on the particular circumstances.[10] Quantz places *Cammer-Ton* a minor third below old *Chor-Ton*.[11]

J. S. Bach's pitches

From surviving sets of parts for Bach's cantatas in Mühlhausen, Weimar, and Leipzig, we can see that the instrumentalists used two different pitches. At Mühlhausen and Leipzig, *Chor-Ton* and *Cammer-Ton* were a whole step apart (this was the most usual situation elsewhere also), and in Weimar they were a minor third apart. The recorders, oboes, and bassoons at Weimar were thus probably at low French chamber pitch. Between 1707 and 1717, Bach's practice was to notate the woodwind parts a whole tone, or sometimes a minor third, higher than the others, in order to accommodate their *Cammer-Ton* pitch to the organ. At Cöthen, there was apparently no difference between *Chor-Ton* and *Cammer-Ton*, since there are no transposed parts for the works performed there. In Leipzig, where

Chor-Ton and *Cammer-Ton* were a whole step apart, Bach and Johann Kuhnau (1660–1722) used another practice for notating parts. The voice, string, and woodwind parts were written in *Cammer-Ton*, whereas the organ, trombone, and often the trumpet parts were notated a tone below that, since their sounding pitch was higher.

During the first quarter of the eighteenth century, other composers, such as Friedrich Wilhelm Zachow (1663–1712) and Kuhnau, also wrote woodwind parts in keys for instruments at low French pitch, but thereafter the use of the higher *Cammer-Ton* is more usual. There was even an attempt by German musicians toward the middle of the century to establish a standard *Cammer-Ton* level, which would be a whole tone below *Chor-Ton*. The common pitches of Bach's day can be summarized as follows:

Chor-Ton (= Praetorius's pitch) $a^1 = 445$–460?
High Cammer-Ton   a whole step lower
Low Cammer-Ton   a minor third lower

With the increasing popularity of French woodwind instruments in Germany after 1700, some new organs were built which played at the lower chamber pitch. Gottfried Silbermann (1683–1753), among others, constructed organs at *Cammer-Ton*, including two that Bach is known to have played in Dresden. It was also possible to bring down the pitch level on an existing organ, but this was a costly solution, since some large pipes had to be added, and there was not always room for them in the organ case. Another solution was to tune a few stops to *Cammer-Ton* pitch, but by far the simplest solution was for the organist to transpose the organ part or copy it out in another key.

Low pitches used in France

Georg Muffat (1653–1704) reports after studying with Lully that French pitch was a whole step lower than ordinary old *Chor-Ton* (or German "cornet" pitch). He observed that the French found that pitch too high, "too squeaky and too forced [*trop piaillant, & trop forcé*];" in their operas, they tuned another half step lower still.[12] Thus, French pitches in use were approximately a whole step below old *Chor-Ton* pitch for chamber music and a minor third below old *Chor-Ton* for the opera.

From Muffat we know that French pitches in common use were equivalent to the two *Cammer-Ton* pitches used in Germany after players brought the French woodwinds there. Quantz also observed that "after the French had transformed the German cross-pipe into the transverse flute, the schawm into the oboe, and the bombard into the bassoon, using their lower and more agreeable pitch, the high choir pitch began in Germany to be supplanted by the chamber pitch."[13]

For the Paris Académie Royale de Musique (called the Opéra), the lower pitch was preferred. Though pitch rose slightly during the eighteenth century in

France, it still remained relatively low compared to that of other cities, probably between a^1, 392 and 420 (modern g^1 is 392). A tuning fork belonging to the harpsichord builder, Pascal Taskin, and tuned for use in the Musique de la Chambre at Versailles, supposedly represented the pitch of the oboe played by François Sallantin in about 1780, and was at $a^1 = 409$.[14] In 1810 the pitch of the Paris Opéra was still only $a^1 = 423$.[15]

Some high and low pitches in Italy

Quantz provides some documentation about pitch levels in Italian cities. In 1752 he wrote:

> At the present time the Venetian pitch is the highest; it is almost the same as our old choir pitch. The Roman pitch of about twenty years ago was low, and was equal to that of Paris. At present, however, the Parisian pitch is beginning almost to equal that of Venice.[16]

Agricola concurs with Quantz, citing Venice and Lombardy for their high pitch, which he says is about a semitone lower than "ordinary choir- or trumpet-pitch." He puts *Cammer-Ton* a minor third below *Chor-Ton* and Roman pitch lower still, "almost like the former French pitch,"[17] or a major third below *Chor-Ton*. It is possible that woodwind players transposed their parts up a step as they did in northern Germany, but string instruments from Cremona were probably made to be played at the higher pitch.

Choosing a pitch for modern performance

Although such differences in pitch may not at first seem crucial to players today, there are some important considerations. The tone of woodwind instruments is markedly different at different pitches. At a higher pitch, the instruments project better and are more brilliant and agile, while the lower-pitched woodwind instruments produce a mellower, softer tone which blends especially well with other instruments. String instruments, too, vary considerably in brightness, sonority, and speed of response depending upon their pitch. Returning a piece to its original pitch level may also ease the vocal register and thus change the sonority significantly.

Various combinations of instruments may pose difficulties and even necessitate substitutions in instrumentation depending upon the pitch and temperament. Many organs built today after historical designs are tuned in unequal temperaments and may play at pitches other than a^1, 440. Harpsichords are often built with the capability of shifting the keyboard to allow it to transpose by a half step, or sometimes by two half steps. Charles Burney described such a harpsichord made in Berlin that was capable of moving two half steps.[18] A historically accurate copy of a flute may play best at a¹, 402, but few other instruments are likely to be available to play with it. For this reason, many builders and players today have adopted a¹, 415, as a useful compromise for most baroque music. In a concert, pitches and temperaments must be chosen carefully, since retuning is often difficult and impractical. The music and its sonority should be the player's ultimate guide.

Equal and nonequal temperaments

When equal temperament is used, there is no difference in pitch between enharmonically equivalent notes (such as E♯ and F). In twentieth-century music and in most pieces that are highly chromatic or that modulate to distant keys, equal temperament is desirable on keyboard instruments in order to make the chromatic or enharmonic shifts possible. Its disadvantage is a lack of any intervals (except the octave) that are pure, and it therefore drew considerable criticism during the eighteenth century. In equal temperament, the major thirds are considerably larger than pure, the fifths are all slightly flatter than perfect, and fourths are sharper. Even though nonequal temperaments restricted the player to fewer keys, they were preferred throughout the baroque era by most performers because they incorporated more pure intervals than equal temperament did and because modulations and dissonances sounded markedly different.

Tuning systems that use the entire octave as the basis for a scale are always tempered in one way or another. On keyboard instruments, for example, it is necessary to temper the intervals within the octave in order to keep the octave in tune. If one begins tuning perfect fifths at middle C, the last fifth that closes the octave C–C circle is E♯–B♯. If one were to tune all the fifths perfect, the B♯ would be slightly sharper than its enharmonic equivalent, C. Twelve perfect fifths are larger than seven octaves by this small interval, which can be expressed as 23.4 cents, or one-ninth of a whole tone. This interval is called the Pythagorean comma. If one tunes pure thirds rather than perfect fifths, the difference is slightly greater. One octave is larger than three pure thirds by an interval called a diesis (41.1 cents). The difference between an octave and four perfect fifths with a pure third is called a syntonic comma (21.5 cents). Tunings with pure thirds also produced a wolf interval, usually between G♯ and E flat (although the tuner could place it elsewhere), which was significantly larger than pure and therefore very dissonant.

Thus in nearly all tuning systems of the seventeenth century or later, the octave is perfect and the syntonic comma is distributed among several intervals within the scale. If the comma is distributed among all twelve semitones, it may be divided into very small parts so that no interval is perfectly in tune but each is slightly out of tune (as in equal temperament). Another solution was to break the circle of fifths and temper some intervals more than others. Certain accidentals were then unavailable to the player. If B flat was tuned as a pure third from D, for example, then A♯ was unusable, because it would be too out of tune to be

acceptable to the ear. On keyboard instruments, this problem of unusable accidentals was sometimes alleviated by providing split keys, so that two different
strings (or pipes, on an organ) could be used. Many keyboard instruments of the
seventeenth century had this feature.

Most baroque temperaments differ in two ways from equal temperament:
(1) some keys in a given temperament cannot be used because they sound much
worse than others, and (2) often some of the thirds are tuned much lower than in
equal temperament so that they sound "pure," without beats.

In the seventeenth century, several types of meantone temperament were
favored that have in common the use of pure (or sometimes slightly tempered)
thirds, and four fifths that are tempered flatter than pure. In a quarter-comma
meantone, for example, the comma is divided between four fifths, and the rest of
the notes of the scale are derived by tuning thirds from these five notes. In this
temperament the player must choose two accidentals according to what the
music requires: either D♯ (tuned pure with B) or E flat (tuned pure with G), and
either A♯ (pure third with F♯, itself pure with D) or B flat (pure with D). The
resulting E flat is higher that D♯, and B flat is higher than A♯. Many seventeenth-
century composers restricted the use of accidentals and wrote in keys with few
sharps or flats in order to enhance the good qualities of meantone temperament,
namely its pure thirds. In his *Organographia* (1619), Praetorius advocates a
quarter-comma meantone for keyboard instruments,[19] and Mersenne also used
it. Other varieties of meantone, such as one-fifth- and one-sixth-comma, had
tempered major thirds, either slightly smaller or larger than pure.

Although meantone was favored in the seventeenth century, other
temperaments that permitted modulations to more keys gained greater use
during the eighteenth century. Many of these temperaments retained some
similarity to meantone by keeping several pure thirds and the four tempered
fifths. In one temperament described by Kirnberger (now called "Kirnberger
III"), the four meantone fifths were retained along with one pure third (C–E).[20]
A few temperaments, such as those described by the theorist Andreas Werckmeister in *Musikalische Temperatur* (1691), permitted modulation to more distant
keys by adjusting intervals and allowing some enharmonic intervals;[21] these
temperaments qualify as "well-tempered," though each semitone is still not
exactly equally spaced as in equal temperament.

Equal temperament was known at least as early as the sixteenth century,
but its use was generally restricted to fretted instruments such as the lute and
viol.[22] Froberger used equal temperament on keyboard instruments, and
according to a report by G. B. Doni in 1647, Frescobaldi also advocated it.[23]
Nevertheless, meantone temperaments remained the preferred ones in the
seventeenth century, and some other irregular temperaments (irregular because
their semitones are of different sizes) were advocated thereafter.

The temperament one chooses for performance is of more than purely
historical interest, for many period instruments—natural (valveless) trumpets
and woodwinds, for example—play more easily in a nonequal temperament.
Others, including fretted instruments such as the lute and viols, can play in equal
temperament, but they can also adapt to other temperaments by adjusting the
frets slightly and by using alternate fingerings for some notes. A piece requiring

either D♯ or E flat and A♯ or B flat (but not both of the enharmonic equivalents) usually works well in meantone temperament, particularly if prominent chords are those with pure thirds. Pieces in minor keys played in meantone temperament may require the addition of a major ("Picardy") third at the ends of sections or at the final cadence, even if it is not specifically indicated, in order to enhance the sonority of the resolution. As with the pitch level, the overriding consideration for players and singers must be how the music sounds in a particular temperament and how well the instruments respond to it.

Bibliographical notes

The literature on pitch and temperament in the baroque era is extensive. A concise, informative summary is presented in the articles "Just Intonation," "Pitch," "Temperament," and "Well-Tempered Clavier," in *Grove*. For an example of a baroque theorist's disapproval of equal temperament, see Johann Philipp Kirnberger, "Equal Temperament," from *Die Kunst des reinen Satzes in der Musik* (Berlin and Konigsberg, 1776–1779), in *Rowen*, 212–213.

In *Lutes, Viols, and Temperaments*, Mark Lindley examines the use of different temperaments on fretted instruments, providing discussions of the music, quotations from theorists, and an excellent bibliography. Arthur Mendel's authoritative article expands his earlier work on the subject, in which he presents an exhaustive investigation, including discussion of vocal ranges, and an extensive bibliography. Two illuminating subsequent studies that challenge some of Mendel's findings are those of Herbert Myers (1984) and Bruce Haynes (1985). The latter is a broad-ranging discussion of pitches in France, Italy, and several German centers. In a subsequent article, Haynes (1986) discusses how pitch differences between instruments affect modern editions and performance.

FOR FURTHER STUDY

Barbour, J. Murray. "Bach and *The Art of Temperament.*" *MQ* 33 no. 1 (January 1947): 67–71.

Blood, William. "'Well-Tempering' the Clavier: Five Methods for Practical Tuning." *EM* 7 (October 1979): 491–495.

Dombois, E. M. "Varieties of Meantone Temperament Realized on the Lute." *JLSA* 7 (1974): 82–89.

Ellis, A. J. "On the History of Musical Pitch." *Journal of the (Royal) Society of Arts* 28 (1880): 293–336, 400–403; 29 (1881): 109–112; for reprint see Mendel.

Haynes, Bruce. "Johann Sebastian Bach's Pitch Standards: the New Perspective." *JAMIS* 11 (1985): 55–114.

———. "Questions of Tonality in Bach's Cantatas: the Woodwind Perspective." *JAMIS* 12 (1986): 40–67.

Jones, Edward Huws. *The Performance of English Song, 1610–1670*. New York: Garland, 1989.

Jorgensen, Owen. *Tuning the Historical Temperaments by Ear*. Marquette: Northern Michigan University Press, 1977.

Klop, G. C. *Harpsichord Tuning*. Transl. Glen Wilson. Garderen, Holland: Werkplaats voor Clavecimbelbouw, 1974.

Lindley, Mark. *Lutes, Viols and Temperaments*. Cambridge: Cambridge University Press, 1984.

———. "Tuning and Intonation." In *Performance Practice: Music after 1600*, 169–185. Ed. Howard Mayer Brown and Stanley Sadie. New York: W. W. Norton and Co., 1989.

———, with Klaus Wachsmann, J. J. K. Rhodes, and W. R. Thomas. "Pitch." *Grove*, 14: 779–786.

Mendel, Arthur. "On the Pitches in Use in Bach's Time," *MQ* 41 (1955): 332–354, 466–480.

———. "Pitch in the Sixteenth and Early Seventeenth Centuries," *MQ* 34 (1948): 28–45, 199–221, 336–357, 575–593.

———. "Pitch in Western Music Since 1500: a Re-Examination." *Acta Musicologica* 50 (1978): 1–93, 328.

———, and A. J. Ellis. *Studies in the History of Musical Pitch* (Amsterdam: Frits Knuf, 1968). (Reprints of previous articles by Mendel ["On the Pitches in Use in Bach's Time" and others] and Ellis).

Meyers, Herbert W. "Praetorius's Pitch." *EM* 12 no. 3 (August 1984): 369–371.

Pirrotta, Antonino. "Temperaments and Tendencies in the Florentine Camerata." Transl. Nigel Fortune. *MQ* 40 no. 2 (1954): 169–189.

Waitzman, Mimi S. "Meantone Temperament in Theory and Practice," *In Theory Only* 5 no. 4 (1979–81): 3–15.

Williams, Peter. "Equal Temperament and the English Organ, 1675–1825," *Acta Musicologica* 40 (1968): 56–65.

NOTES TO CHAPTER 4

1. Playford, *An Introduction to the Skill of Musick*, 107.
2. *Quantz*, 31–32.
3. *Quantz*, 267.
4. Adlung, *Musica mechanica organoedi*, v. 2, 55.
5. Praetorius, *De organographia* (New York: Broude, 1966), 16–17, and Tables 37–38.
6. Mendel, "Pitch in Western Music since 1500," 76.
7. Myers, "Praetorius's Pitch," 370; Haynes, "Bach's Pitch Standard," 60.
8. Cary Karp, "Pitch," in *Performance Practice: Music after 1600*, ed. Howard Mayer Brown and Stanley Sadie (New York: W. W. Norton and Co., 1989), 157. Using similar evidence about possible shrinkage of Praetorius's paper, Mark Lindley and Klaus Wachsmann suggest that *Chor-Ton* may have been closer to a^1, 425, or about three-fifths of a semitone below modern a^1 (*Grove*, "Pitch," v. 14, p. 780).
9. Haynes, 64.
10. Kuhnau, quoted by Johann Mattheson, *Critica musica* (Hamburg, 1725) v. 2, 235. See Haynes, 59–60.
11. *Quantz*, 268.
12. Muffat, preface to *Florilegium secundum* (1698), in Walter Kolneder, *Georg Muffat zur Aufführungspraxis* (Strasbourg: Éditions P. H. Heitz, 1970), 73.
13. *Quantz*, 267.
14. Haynes, 105.
15. J. J. K. Rhodes and W. R. Thomas, "Pitch," in *Grove*, v. 14, 785.
16. *Quantz*, 267.
17. Agricola, *Anleitung zur Singkunst*, 45. See Haynes, 83f.
18. Burney, *The Present State of Music*, 189.

19. Praetorius, *De organographia* (New York: Broude, 1966), 145.
20. See Kirnberger, *The Art of Strict Composition*, transl. David Beach and Jürgen Thym.
21. Temperaments by Werckmeister, Kirnberger, and others are illustrated in G. C. Klop, *Harpsichord Tuning*, transl. Glen Wilson (Garderen, Holland: Werkplaats voor Clavicimbelbouw, 1974), 18ff.
22. On other temperaments for fretted instruments (such as meantone and Valotti), see Appendix I, "Tuning," by Elisabeth Liddle, in Alison Crum's *Play the Viol* (Oxford: Oxford University Press, 1989), 155–164.
23. Lindley, "Temperament," *Grove*, v. 18, p. 665.

5

The Basso Continuo

The basso continuo is the core of most baroque solo and ensemble music. Its beginnings coincide with the new attitudes and expressive ideals of the Florentine Camerata at the end of the sixteenth century. Gradually its rhythmic and harmonic support became a necessary addition for most combinations of instruments and voices. Composers used a conventional shorthand notation with numbers (called figures) written above or below the bass line to indicate the appropriate harmonies. With this bass line, chordal instruments improvised an accompaniment, called a "realization," according to certain conventions and the player's own taste.

The choice of instruments was sometimes indicated by the composer, but frequently the performers had to determine which instruments were most appropriate for the particular environment and musical forces involved. The harpsichord, organ, lute, chitarrone (a lute with extra bass strings, also called a theorbo), guitar, harp, and sometimes the viola da gamba were used as chordal instruments for the basso continuo. Sustaining instruments such as the bassoon, violoncello, viola da gamba, and sackbut often doubled the bass line. The conventions associated with the basso continuo in opera, chamber, and church music differed over certain periods and in some geographic locales. Individual composers, too, placed different demands upon the continuo. Thus, when performing baroque music, one should attempt to identify both the number and type of instruments for the basso continuo, and also to find an appropriate manner of realizing the part provided by the composer.

Use and function of the continuo in the seventeenth century

The improvisatory chordal practice embodied in basso continuo playing may be traced to secular origins in the sixteenth century. The lute, viola da braccio, lirone (a viola da gamba with nine to fourteen strings, also called lira da gamba), harpsichord, or any chordal instrument supplied a repeating progression of chordal harmonies over one of the ostinato patterns such as a descending tetrachord (called the passacaglia) as an accompaniment to singing or even to the recitation of an epic poem. Other functions of an improvised accompaniment were largely practical: to keep a group of singers on pitch, or to replace instruments that were not available, as, for example, in certain church services.

The earliest example of a separate printed basso continuo part is found in Giovanni Croce's *Motetti a otto voci* (Venice, 1594).[1] Early basso continuo parts in sacred music evidently served either for a polychoral setting, as in Croce's music, or as an accompaniment to monody, as in Lodovico Viadana's *Cento concerti ecclesiastici* (Op. 12, 1602), which are for one to four voices and continuo.

A transition toward the use of a basso continuo in secular music was the inclusion of a continuo part in Monteverdi's *Madrigali*, Book 5 (Venice, 1605). Although a separate partbook was provided for the player, the bass line is independent of the voices in only a few works; in general, it follows a *basso seguente* practice, in which the bass line is formed from the lowest sounding voice.

The introduction of the basso continuo part parallels the development of the new style of singing advocated by Caccini in his *Le nuove musiche* (1602). The new expressive ideal in singing was a solo voice supported by the chordal harmony of a continuo instrument—for Caccini, ideally the theorbo or chitarrone—on which the player improvised an accompaniment from the notated bass line. Caccini provides only a few figures, primarily a ♯ or 4–♯3, or its equivalent, 11–♯10, indicating the intervallic distance of the notes above the bass. The texture and rhythm of the accompaniment are left to the player, who is instructed to discreetly leave the singer free to apply a certain "noble neglect of the rhythm" in order to express the meaning of the text.

The "noble neglect of the rhythm" and expressive use of dynamics and ornamentation advocated by Caccini became associated with the new recitative style [*stile recitativo*] which occupied a central position in large-scale dramatic works, such as Caccini's opera *Euridice* (1600) and Monteverdi's operas. The basso continuo appears in instrumental music slightly later than in vocal music. In the solo sonatas and trios of Cima and Castello, there is evidence of the transfer of recitative style and ornamentation from vocal music to purely instrumental music.

Music of the early baroque, from about 1600 to 1650, was usually performed with a single chordal continuo instrument, such as the harpsichord, lute (or its relatives, the theorbo, archlute, and chitarrone), or the organ. A sustaining bass instrument, such as the cello or bassoon, was not usually added unless a separate (and usually more elaborate) part was written for it. In the latter case, as in an Italian sonata with violins, the motion of the independent bass part for the cello usually coincides with the violins; that is, it plays or rests whenever they do. It functions, therefore, as one of the strings rather than as a doubling instrument for the continuo line. This is the usual practice in most early baroque music, both sacred and secular, although in opera and oratorio the continuo may have been supported by the addition of a cello and a lute with extra bass strings (archlute or chitarrone) in order to provide more support for the singers. In the air, "Possente spirto," from Monteverdi's *Orfeo* (see Appendix A), the composer indicates that Orfeo should sing to the accompaniment of "an organ with wooden pipes and a chitarrone."

After 1680 or thereabouts, doubling of the bass line by a sustaining instrument was more prevalent, though still not obligatory. The increased rhythmic and melodic importance of the bass line gave it equal prominence in chamber cantatas and sonatas. The most frequent combinations were a harpsichord and either viola da gamba or cello (the latter being called *violone* in early seventeenth-century printed sources). In Italian sacred music the bassoon and trombone are rarely used as bass solo instruments after 1650, but the bassoon remains an important basso continuo instrument in north-German contexts, as in the music of Buxtehude and Bach, for example. The bassoon is also frequently prescribed in French opera, where it usually joins the basso continuo whenever oboes are present, either in vocal airs or in instrumental music.

The choice of continuo instruments in French music

In French instrumental music and cantatas, the accompaniment, usually called *basse continue*, may be played by a harpsichord alone, but one or more bowed instruments were generally added as well, whether specifically mentioned or not. Even when a violoncello or viola da gamba is not specified in the printed score, some collections of individual parts for the same piece may specify one or the other, and they may include a separate part for it in addition to that for the harpsichord. Theorbo may also be suitable as a continuo instrument instead of (or even in addition to) harpsichord in some French cantatas, since it was a favored continuo instrument during the first two decades of the eighteenth century.

There is some evidence, largely from the figuring present in manuscript and printed sources, that in French operas by Lully, Rameau, and others the harpsichord played only with solo voices. Following close examination of the figuring practices in harpsichord parts, Graham Sadler concluded that the harpsichord possibly accompanied airs and sections of choruses that were sung by solo voices, but did not play in other choral and instrumental sections, including the ouverture. Jérome de la Gorce has also observed that Lully's continuo group and that for the Opéra until 1704 included about ten players (two harpsichordists, four lute and theorbo players, two viol players, and one or two *basses de violons*); after 1704, however, their number was cut in half. Surviving sets of parts show that about half of the continuo group did not play in the ouverture, choruses, and most dances.[2] It therefore seems likely that both harpsichord and theorbo realized the continuo along with several violas da gamba for much of the vocal music in Lully's works. However, the use of the theorbo declined after 1704 until it was suppressed between 1730 and 1735. During the first half of the eighteenth century, the *petit choeur*, an ensemble including the continuo instruments (principally harpsichord and cellos by this time) together with two or three violins and flutes, accompanied the recitative and some vocal airs.

The continuo instruments in Bach's music

In Bach's church music, the organ was of central importance as an accompaniment instrument. Whether the harpsichord was used in some situations in addition to, or instead of, the organ has been a controversial issue among scholars. A recent reexamination of the evidence by Laurence Dreyfus points toward a solution to this perplexing problem. He concludes that Bach used a system of dual accompaniment, in which the cantatas performed in the Thomas-Kirche and Nikolai-Kirche in Leipzig (1723–1750) were accompanied by the harpsichord,[3] largely for the practical reason that the harpsichordist could communicate more easily than the organist with the other players, since the organist's back was always to the orchestra. In both large and small works there is considerable evidence that both harpsichord and organ realized the continuo (usually joined by a cello, bassoon, and sometimes a violone). Evidence for the specific parts that were played by the organ or the harpsichord in Bach's music can be gathered from the notated pitch of the surviving parts. Since organs were built at the higher *Chor-Ton* pitch, their parts were transposed lower than those of the harpsichord and the other instruments that played at *Cammer-Ton* pitch. With this evidence as a foundation, it seems likely that Bach's practice was one in which the two instruments played simultaneously, hence the term dual accompaniment. In Bach's pre-Weimar compositions (before 1714), the continuo practice was closer to earlier seventeenth-century practice, in which the cello joined the organ only in some movements.[4] The frequent, but incorrect, modern practice of accompanying the choruses and other full-textured pieces in Bach's Passions with organ, alternating with harpsichord in the lightly scored arias, owes its origin to C. P. E. Bach (1762), who described this practice for use in pieces of a light, thin texture.[5]

Realizing the continuo part

The practices of continuo realization, largely an improvisatory art, were learned by virtually every keyboard player in the baroque era. Since these practices differ for each repertory and according to geography and period, players must consider questions not only about the meaning of the figures themselves, but also about texture, arpeggiation, dissonance, register, and ornamentation for each composer and type of music. The individual styles of continuo playing are definable to a certain extent with the help of various kinds of historical evidence, but the player must rely upon these only as a starting point from which experimentation and knowledge of the literature will lead to idiomatic and personal realizations.

The historical evidence is of at least three types: (1) theoretical treatises on how to realize continuo parts, (2) surviving examples of written-out continuo parts, and (3) written accounts and observations about continuo players and their performances. For the choice of instruments that double the bass line, the additional evidence of surviving parts indicating which instruments actually played, as well as some visual depictions of continuo groups, also add valuable information to the written historical evidence.

SEVENTEENTH-CENTURY TREATISES ON CONTINUO PLAYING

Two early sources for accompanying in the Italian style are the preface to Lodovico Grossi da Viadana's *Cento concerti ecclesiastici* (Venice, 1602) and Agazzari's *Del suonare sopra il basso con tutti stromenti & uso loro nel conserto* (Siena, 1607).[6] They advocate an organ accompaniment that is discreet and elegant, with suitable decorations especially when the voice or voices rest. The range in which the accompanist plays is of concern to both writers, and they advise remaining below the singers as much as possible. Agazzari also warns against playing the same notes that the soprano is singing, and he recommends avoiding the upper register altogether. Viadana, on the contrary, cites an exception to the general rule of remaining below the singers, namely in the accompaniment of a piece whose register or tessitura is high. Here he recommends not playing too low in the accompaniment. Both writers agree that the part should remain simple, especially in the left hand. Although these early principles do not prescribe exactly how the chords are to be played, they do suggest the boundaries of taste for accompanying sacred music on the organ. These principles are suitable for accompanying early seventeenth-century Italian music as well as sacred music by composers who wrote in a similar style, such as Heinrich Schütz.

Agazzari also describes the function of various continuo instruments in a large ensemble as one of either foundation or ornamentation. Instruments that provide a foundation "guide and sustain" the entire group; these are the harpsichord, organ, and in an ensemble with one or a few voices, also the lute, theorbo, or harp. Ornamental instruments were those that played moving lines and counterpoints, making the harmony "agreeable and sonorous" by improvising an accompaniment from the figured bass. Among the instruments of this type, he names several plucked instruments (lute, theorbo, cither, chitarrone, and bandora), as well as the lirone and spinet (a small harpsichord). Evidently some instruments could be used in either function, because his list of ornamental instruments includes several that he also named as foundation instruments.

The principle that the basso continuo part should remain discreet and simple is repeated in several treatises, especially in the seventeenth century. Among English writers who also ascribed to this rule were Matthew Locke, whose *Melothesia or certain general rules for playing upon a continued-bass* was published in London in 1673.[7] When the bass moves quickly, he advises that the right hand play only at the beginning and middle of each measure. A manuscript treatise by John Blow (B.M. Add. 34072, ff 1–5) from about the same time consists of directions for playing from a "Through'-Bass" on a harpsichord or organ, in which he illustrates the common chordal progressions.[8] Like Locke's treatise, it was evidently intended primarily for teaching purposes. Blow recommends that if the bass moves by eighth or sixteenth notes, the right hand should play only once per quarter note.

Also written primarily as pedagogical tools were several German treatises, such as Andreas Werckmeister's *Die nothwendigsten Anmerkungen und Regeln wie der Bassus continuus oder General-Bass wohl könne tractiret werden* (Aschersleben, 1698).[9] He writes that ordinarily "with each bass note, the eighth, fifth, and third are taken" (in other words, one normally plays root position chords on each bass note). Figures were used to alter the harmonies, according to Werckmeister. When a 6 or 7 is written, one ordinarily leaves out the fifth, and when a 2 or 4 is written, one leaves out the third. Whenever possible, contrary motion should be introduced between the bass and right hand. He also endorses the important principle that one should not merely play exactly what is written in the figures, but instead carefully avoid doubling dissonances that are already being heard. Thus, the figures represent the harmonies of the composition, but do not imply that every figure must be realized by the player.

Published only two years after Werckmeister's treatise, Friedrich Erhard Niedt's *Musicalische Handleitung* (Hamburg, 1700) illustrates the preparation of dissonances such as the seventh degree.[10] When the figure 7 is present, according to Niedt, the seventh is always prepared, but when the figure $\frac{7}{3}$ appears, the seventh is not prepared and the chord is simply struck. His examples illustrate that the texture may alternate between three- and four-part harmony, with one note in the bass and two or three in the right hand.

EIGHTEENTH-CENTURY TREATISES ON CONTINUO PLAYING

One of the most important German treatises from the first half of the eighteenth century, Heinichen's *Der General-Bass in der Composition* (Dresden, 1728) provides a useful guide to interpreting Bach's continuo parts. He tells the player how to realize harmonies when the bass notes are fully figured, partially figured, and even when there are no figures at all.[11] According to Heinichen, the accompanist may be confronted with "arias, cantatas, operas, instrumental solos, duets, &c" in which the bass is not figured. In such cases, the harmony must be inferred from the score, or from a single part above the bass line. In order to aid the player in acquiring this skill, he provides examples of the common progressions and resolutions. He mentions the permissibility of certain irregularities, particularly in opera or in the theatrical style (as opposed to the chamber or church styles), that is to say, in large-scale performances where details of voice leading would not easily be heard. He advocated some freedom in the preparation of dissonances, for example, and he observed that the principles of harmonic motion were most abused in recitative. He also includes an account of the *acciaccatura* based upon that of Gasparini, as discussed in the next section.

In recitatives, the bass notes were usually written in tied whole and half notes, but there is considerable theoretical evidence to suggest that the notes were shortened in performance to about the value of a quarter note, and that another chord was restruck only at a change of harmony. In accompanied recitative (in which the upper strings joined the continuo), long notes were usually played as written. In the recitative, "Zwar fühlt mein schwaches Herz Furcht," from Bach's *Liebster Gott, wenn werd ich sterben* (BWV 8, Appendix A), for example, the notes in the continuo part should be sustained along with those of the strings. This practice was widely accepted throughout the eighteenth century by German and Italian players, as theoretical evidence from Heinichen, Niedt, and others shows.[12] Telemann advocates a slightly different practice, that of sustaining the bass on the harpsichord when the harmony changes several times above it, while releasing each chord in the right hand successively.[13]

Only a few fragments of actual written-out continuo realizations survive. One example is a basso continuo part in the hand of Christian Friedrich Penzel for Bach's aria, "Empfind' ich Höllenangst und Pein" (BWV 3), which dates from about 1770.[14] It is predominantly in four parts (with three notes in the right hand and the bass note in the left). It also adheres to two other important principles: (1) chords need not be supplied on every note of the bass, and (2) the right hand ought to remain near the bass most of the time and rarely be more than an octave away from it.

ITALIAN CONTINUO PLAYING

Several treatises that describe Italian continuo practices of the late seventeenth and early eighteenth centuries, such as those by Pasquini, Gasparini, Geminiani, Pasquali, and others, deal specifically with the harpsichord. On an Italian harpsichord, with its bright attack and quick decay, especially in the treble part of the instrument, it was necessary to introduce dissonances and ornamentation, and to repeat notes and chords in order to produce a full sound that would provide enough foundation for singers. Several Italian writers speak of *acciaccature*, or "crushed" combinations of dissonances and their resolution, which are struck simultaneously. *Acciaccature* are also found in the harpsichord solos of Domenico Scarlatti and were evidently used frequently in continuo playing, especially in recitatives.

Francesco Gasparini (*L'armonico pratico al cembalo*, 1708) warns that a player should avoid too much arpeggiation in continuo playing by reserving it mainly for consonant chords.[15] He describes a manner of filling in notes of a triad with a dissonant tone, a technique he finds especially useful for a minor chord (presumably to fill in the notes between the tonic and minor third). One can, he says, also add a half step below the root of a chord in first inversion. This type of filler he calls a mordent (from *mordente*, or "biting") because it resembles "the bite of a small animal that releases its hold as soon as it bites, and so does no harm." In addition to decorating the third of a chord, this dissonance may be used especially on the octave or sixth of a chord. The more complicated dissonance called the *acciaccatura* consists of two, three, or four notes struck with a chord and released, an effect useful in recitatives and in serious airs, according to Gasparini. These are essential effects for making the accompaniment "harmonious and delightful," but he does not elaborate upon the frequency of their use. Gasparini, like several earlier writers, advises that one should never play "note for note" the same melody that is played by the upper part.

Francesco Geminiani (*A Treatise of Good Taste in the Art of Musick*, London, 1749) offers an explanation and example of how one might arpeggiate in accompanying and how to add *acciaccature* (Example 5-1). He marks notes in black which the right hand should release immediately, sometimes including several dissonant notes within a single chord, as in measure 4.

Example 5-1. Francesco Geminiani, How to arpeggiate and use *acciaccature* in the continuo, from *A Treatise of Good Taste in the Art of Musick* (London, 1749).

Among the surviving accounts of observers who witnessed eighteenth-century performances, there are numerous references to continuo players. Charles de Brosses, who observed opera performances in Rome and elsewhere during a trip to Italy in 1739 and 1740, found the accompaniment of the basso continuo to be "very simple, only providing one note during the rests between the phrases to sustain the tone; the harpsichord plays in a rough way [*une manière rude*] and never plays arpeggios."[16] Other French writers echo de Brosses in observing that Italian players toward the middle of the eighteenth century arpeggiated less than they had evidently done about a half century earlier, and in reporting their strokes as brisk and regular.

FRENCH CONTINUO PLAYING

A few seventeenth-century sources deal with figured bass playing on the theorbo, but one of the earliest to include the harpsichord is Denis Delair's *Traité de l'accompagnement sur le théorbe et le clavecin* (Paris, 1690). His comments are general rather than specific, since they are intended for both the harpsichordist and the theorbo player. He cites two important principles: (1) chords may be "filled in" with nonharmonic tones for greater sonority, and (2) the texture should vary according to the tempo of individual passages. He describes two ways of accompanying on the harpsichord, one in which chords are played with the right hand and the bass with the left, and the other in which chords are played with both hands. He prefers the former method for pieces whose bass line moves quickly, and the latter for use in slow tempos.

D'Anglebert (*Principes de l'accompagnement*, 1689) agrees that chords can be filled in with both hands when the tempo is slow. His examples show chords of close spacing and full sonority, with the left hand occasionally playing only one note but more frequently three or even four notes, while the right hand adds three or four more (Example 5-2). He also illustrates the manner of "filling in" the harmony suggested by Delair: one arpeggiates a chord and adds appoggiaturas consisting of nonharmonic tones, which are then released while the chord is held.

Example 5-2. J.-H. d'Anglebert, The manner of accompanying, from *Principes de l'accompagnement* (1689).

Michel de Saint Lambert (*Les principes du clavecin*, Paris, 1702) also supports the foregoing principles. The harpsichordist should adjust the texture of the accompaniment to the number of instruments and voices being accompanied. In choruses, one may repeat chords at will for greater rhythmic support and volume. In recitatives, Saint Lambert recommends arpeggiating chords in general, sometimes restriking them or repeating only one or two notes. His examples, like those of d'Anglebert, demonstrate that variety of texture was the essence of the French style of accompaniment, with thicker chords to provide more support and accent on stressed words or syllables, and only a few notes for less important chords that pass quickly. There is evidence from another observer, Bonnot de Mably, that the French style of accompaniment gradually became more complicated [*tumultueux*] than it had been in Lully's day,[17] possibly in response to the gradual slowing down of the speed of delivery of French recitative from about 1680 to 1740.

Thomas-Louis Bourgeois (1676–1750 or 1751) provides one of the few directions for registration in harpsichord continuo passages. For a delicate air from his cantata *Psiché* with obbligato viol, Bourgeois specifies the upper manual on the harpsichord to accompany the obbligato viol (or flute) and soprano (Example 5-3), but he reserves this change of manual for one air, the only one in the cantata which uses an obbligato instrument. Michel Corrette also mentions the use of the upper manual and suggests using it to accompany recitative by Italian composers in order to produce a softer sound [*sans faire beaucoup de bruit*].[18]

Example 5-3. Thomas-Louis Bourgeois, "Revenez cher amant," air from *Psiché* (*Cantates*, Book 2 [Paris, 1718]), with indication for use of the upper manual on the harpsichord.

Jean Henri d'Anglebert also mentions the use of organ as a continuo instrument in his *Principes* of 1689.[19] He advises the use of a four-part harmonic style for organ accompaniment, with one note in the left hand and three in the right hand. He and other writers agree that the organ accompaniment should in general be simpler than that played on a harpsichord. The player should avoid a leaping [*sautillante*] style of accompaniment and instead should join chords smoothly, paying attention to voice leading. Arpeggios and ornamentation are rare in organ accompaniment.

In the eighteenth century, similar principles of accompaniment remained current in France. Laurent Gervais (fl. 1725–1745), a harpsichordist, teacher, and composer from Rouen who settled in Paris, published a treatise on continuo playing in 1733 with the following advice:

> One must put the chords into a register of the keyboard that is proportionate to that of the basso continuo; that is to say, the chords should not be too near, nor too far away from it, and one must foresee the movement of the bass line, so that the right hand is only disrupted when absolutely necessary.
>   One should not lift the right hand without noticing that there is almost always a note from the chord one is leaving that belongs to

the chord which follows; thus, it is better to make the fingers pass smoothly from one chord to the other, so that by this means the harmony may be more connected [*liée*]. One should even arpeggiate the chords a little, that is to say, play the notes one after the other, with an equal speed [*un mouvement égal*], beginning with the note nearest the bass. This type of accompaniment is used in recitatives, and tender or graceful airs. When one accompanies fast pieces, or large *symphonies*, such as concertos, it is better to strike the chords all at once, and even to double some of them with the left hand as much as one can; the accompaniment cannot be too full on such occasions.[20]

Gervais notes that the right hand thumb is rarely used when accompanying, an observation repeated by Michel Corrette in *Prototipes contenant des leçons d'accompagnement pour servir d'addition au livre intitulé le maître de clavecin* (Paris, 1775). At least, Corrette advises, one should not use the thumb to double the note played by the little finger, "because one never doubles dissonances" (Corrette 1775, 14). For accompanying an *air italien* or other solo vocal piece, Corrette recommends putting the right hand on the upper manual. In recitative, however, one can play more notes, filling out the harmony with chords in both hands, especially when the chords are consonant. He recommends not bringing the right hand too low on the organ, because the chords may be "too obscure." On the organ, too, one may place the right and left hands on different keyboards to differentiate the bass line and accompaniment (Corrette 1775, 15).

Summary and modern considerations

As the core of virtually all vocal and instrumental performances, the basso continuo had an extremely important role in baroque music. The sensitive harpsichordist or organist who adjusts the texture and range of the continuo part, and provides discreet rhythmic and harmonic support without interfering with the soloists, lends a security and firmness to the ensemble that is felt by all. The cello, viola da gamba, double bass, or bassoon, as sustaining instruments, reinforce the bass through subtle melodic, rhythmic, and dynamic shaping of the line. They form a close relationship with the keyboard player, and for this reason the continuo players are usually seated near one another. A painting by John Theodore Heins (1697–1756) of an informal musical gathering (Figure 2) shows such a group, in which the cello and double bass players share the same part near the harpsichord, in the middle of the ensemble.[21]

In the early baroque period, it was customary to use a single chordal instrument for the continuo, and a melodic bass instrument usually was not used unless there was a separate part for it. Whenever possible, root position chords were played, unless the solo part or a figure implied otherwise. The texture of the continuo part varied, especially when played at the harpsichord, whose dynamics could be adjusted to an extent by the number of notes played and the speed of arpeggiation.

Figure 2. John Theodore Heins (1697–1756), "The Astley Family and Friends at Melton Constable, A Musical Party."

Baroque theorists frequently recommend that one should not exceed the range of the solo part, and that in general one should remain in a relatively low register, rarely moving more than an octave above the bass line. French writers in particular stress the importance of staying near the left hand and filling in notes of the harmony with both hands. In this way it was possible to use the characteristically rich tenor register of the French harpsichord to best advantage. Two principle ways of accompanying developed during the first half of the eighteenth century: the French style with its relatively thick texture, low register, and frequent use of arpeggiation, and the Italian style, with some arpeggiation (probably less than in the French style) and more frequent use of dissonances such as the *acciaccatura*. From seventeenth- and eighteenth-century treatises, we know that styles of continuo playing varied in different places at least as much as the practices of ornamentation and articulation did, and there was considerable room for individuality within the boundaries of good taste.

In performing baroque music today, especially from a modern edition, the keyboard player may encounter a written-out realization provided by the editor. Since it is not possible for an editor to provide a realization that serves equally well for harpsichord and organ, or indeed to anticipate the different conditions that may arise in performance, players will find it necessary, at the very least, to adapt the written-out part from time to time. The realization should be carefully examined according to the foregoing principles of range, motion, and texture of the part. In some poor editions, the figures may have been omitted, and the continuo part may depart radically from what may be considered stylistically appropriate. Fortunately, the availability of scholarly performing editions usually gives players the opportunity to choose the best realization from several possibilities; some editions include simple harmonic realizations upon which a player may elaborate. If no realization is available, or if the player wishes to write or improvise one, the figures can be written on a score or a cello part for use at the keyboard. Players who wish to learn the art of improvisation practiced during the baroque era will find numerous treatises and instruction books, and trying out these principles in a variety of performing situations will certainly prove to be a challenging and rewarding way of learning more about it.

Bibliographical notes

There is a wealth of information on continuo playing in the baroque era, including numerous treatises published in facsimile. The list of sources in Appendix C cites some of these. F. T. Arnold's two-volume study of continuo treatises is exhaustive, an indispensable reference tool. Hermann Keller's manual provides a useful summary of the principles of continuo playing, with citations from original sources and many musical examples. The portion of Heinichen's treatise *Der General-Bass in der Composition* dealing with theatrical style is in Buelow's translation (see Appendix C under Heinichen), pp. 381–438.

Important contributions to the history of continuo playing, especially on the instruments used, are the studies by Tharald Borgir and Stephen Bonta listed below. Luigi Tagliavini discusses early Italian harpsichord playing, the use of arpeggiation and ornamentation, and continuo playing on the organ and chitarrone. For evidence taken from existing continuo parts, see the article by John Hill, which includes transcriptions of fully written-out realizations in lute tablatures and for keyboard, and a discussion of dissonance and texture in Caccini's songs.

Graham Sadler's approach in studying surviving harpsichord parts and printed scores yields new thought on when the instrument did not play. Sandra Mangsen counters with evidence that players routinely played from unfigured basses, and the question of when the harpsichord played, especially in opera, remains an open one. Judith Milhouse and Curtis Price document English practice, in which harpsichord was used for large musical productions. Winton Dean discusses Handel's use of two harpsichords (which he apparently initiated in England), observed by a French traveler, Fougeroux.

Because the size and disposition of a continuo group is dependent upon the composition of the entire ensemble, studies of various orchestras and of specific composers' practices also enter the subject of the basso continuo. Laurence Dreyfus presents the results of research on Bach's parts as well as contemporary theoretical evidence. Neal Zaslaw includes a useful bibliography related to regions and composers. Hans Joachim Marx illustrates an orchestral setup for Pasquini (1687), and Ortrun Landmann discusses the historical size of the Dresden Hofkapelle in comparison with other eighteenth-century ensembles.

FOR FURTHER STUDY

Arnold, F. T. *The Art of Accompaniment from a Thorough-Bass as Practised in the Seventeenth and Eighteenth Centuries*. London: Oxford University Press, 1931. R (2 v.) New York: Dover, 1965.

Bonta, Stephen. "The Use of Instruments in Sacred Music in Italy 1560–1700." *EM* 18 (1990): 519–535.

Borgir, Tharald. *The Performance of the Basso Continuo in Italian Baroque Music*. UMI Studies in Musicology, no. 90. Ann Arbor: UMI Research Press, 1987.

Buelow, George J. "Symposium on Seventeenth-Century Music Theory: Germany." *JMT* 16 (1972): 36–49.

Cyr, Mary. "Declamation and Expressive Singing in Recitative." In *Opera and Vivaldi*, ed. Michael Collins and Elise K. Kirk, 233–257. Austin: University of Texas Press, 1984.

Dean, Winton. "A French Traveller's View of Handel Operas." *ML* 55 (1974): 172–178.

Dreyfus, Laurence. *Bach's Continuo Group: Players and Practices in his Vocal Works*. Cambridge, MA: Harvard University Press, 1987.

Garnsey, Sylvia. "The Use of Hand-Plucked Instruments in the Continuo Body: Nicola Matteis." *ML* 47 (1966): 135–140.

Hill, John Walter. "Realized Continuo Accompaniments from Florence c 1600." *EM* 11 no. 2 (April 1983): 194–208.

Horsley, Imogene. "Communication" [on a continuo realization of Corelli's Op. 5 by Antonio Tonelli]. *JAMS* 23 (1970): 545–546.

Keller, Hermann. *Schule des Generalbassspiels* Kassel: Bärenreiter, 1931; second ed., 1950. Transl. Carl Parrish as *Thoroughbass Method*. New York: Norton, 1965.

Landmann, Ortrun. "The Dresden Hofkapelle During the Lifetime of Johann Sebastian Bach." *EM* 17 no. 1 (February 1989): 17–30.

Ledbetter, David. *Continuo Playing According to Handel*. Early Music Series, No. 12. Oxford: OUP, 1989.

Mangsen, Sandra. "The Unfigured Bass and the Continuo Player: More Evidence from France." *Early Keyboard Journal* 3 (1984–1985): 5–12.

Marx, Hans Joachim. "The Instrumentation of Handel's Early Italian Works." *EM* 16 no. 4 (November 1988): 496–505.

Milhouse, Judith, and Curtis Price. "Harpsichords in the London Theatres, 1697–1715." *EM* 18 (February 1990): 38–46.

North, Nigel. *Continuo Playing on the Lute, Archlute and Theorbo*. Bloomington: Indiana University Press, 1987.

Rogers, Patrick J. *Continuo Realization in Handel's Vocal Music*. UMI Studies in Musicology no. 104. Ann Arbor: UMI Research Press, 1989.

Rose, Gloria. "A Fresh Clue from Gasparini on Embellished Figured-Bass Accompaniment." *MT* 107 (1966): 28–29.

Sadler, Graham. "The Role of the Keyboard Continuo in French Opera 1673–1776." *EM* 8 (April 1980): 148–157.

Spitzer, John. "The Birth of the Orchestra in Rome—an Iconographic Study." *EM* 19 (February 1991): 9–27.

Tagliavini, Luigi Ferdinando. "The Art of 'Not Leaving the Instrument Empty.'" *EM* 11 (July 1983): 299–308.

Williams, Peter. "Basso Continuo on the Organ." *ML* 50 (1969): 136–152, 230–245.
_____ . "The Harpsichord Acciaccatura: Theory and Practice in Harmony, 1650–1750."
    MQ 54 (1968): 503–523.
_____ . *Figured Bass Accompaniment.* Edinburgh: Edinburgh University Press, 1970.
Zaslaw, Neal. "When is an Orchestra not an Orchestra?" *EM* 16 (November 1988): 483–
    495.

NOTES TO CHAPTER 5

1. Tharald Borgir, *The Performance of the Basso Continuo* (Ann Arbor: UMI Research
    Press, 1987), 11.
2. Jérôme de la Gorce, "L'orchestre de l'Opéra et son évolution de Campra à Rameau,"
    Revue de musicologie 76:1 (1990), 23–43. See also the same author's "Some Notes
    on Lully's Orchestra," in *Jean-Baptistie Lully and the Music of the French Baroque:
    Essays in Honor of James R. Anthony*, ed. John Hajdu Heyer (Cambridge: Cambridge
    University Press, 1989), 99–112.
3. Dreyfus, *Bach's Continuo Group* (see bibliography for this chapter), 11ff.
4. Dreyfus, 132ff.
5. C. P. E. Bach, *Essay on the True Art*, 172; see Dreyfus, 58.
6. Both prefaces in F. T. Arnold, *The Art of Accompaniment*, v. 1, pp. 2–5, 9–33, and 67–74.
    Viadana's preface is also in *Strunk*, 419–423; Agazzari is in *MacClintock*, 131–132.
7. Arnold, v. 1, pp. 154–163. Facs. of "General rules for playing on a continued bass" in
    Matthew Locke, *Melothesia* (London, 1673), ed. Christopher Hogwood (Oxford:
    Oxford University Press: 1987), x–xvii.
8. Arnold, 163–172.
9. Arnold, 202–213.
10. Arnold, 213–236.
11. George J. Buelow, *Thorough-Bass Accompaniment according to Johann David Heinichen*,
    revised ed. Studies in Musicology no. 86 (UMI Research Press: Ann Arbor, c.
    1986), 219–236. Also in Arnold, v. 1, 255–269.
12. See Dreyfus, 78–88.
13. Telemann, *Singe-, Spiel- und Generalbass-Übungen* (1733–34), 39–40.
14. Reproduced in the introduction to Bach, *The St. John Passion*, ed. Arthur Mendel, xxix.
    The part was formerly thought to be in Bach's hand; see Robert L. Marshall,
    "Authentic Performance: Musical Text, Performing Forces, Performance Style (A
    Review Essay)," in *The Music of Johann Sebastian Bach: the Sources, the Style, the
    Significance* (New York: Schirmer Books, 1989), 229–239. 15. Arnold, 250–255.
16. Charles de Brosses, *Lettres familières écrites d'Italie en 1739 et 1740*, second ed. (Paris,
    1836), v. 2, p. 331.
17. Bonnot de Mably, *Lettres à Madame la Marquise de P . . . sur l'opéra* (Paris, 1741), 152–
    153.
18. Michel Corrette, *Le maître de clavecin pour l'accompagnement, méthode théorique et
    pratique* (Paris, 1753), 91.
19. In J.-H. d'Anglebert, *Pièces de clavecin*, ed. Kenneth Gilbert (Paris: Heugel, n.d.), 138–
    145.
20. [Laurent] Gervais, *Méthode pour l'accompagnement du clavecin* (Paris, [1733]), 27. The
    translation is mine.
21. For a discussion of this painting and others portraying an informal "musical party,"
    see Richard D. Leppert, "Men, Women, and Music at Home: the Influence of
    Cultural Values on Musical Life in Eighteenth-Century England," *Imago musicae* 2
    (1985), 51–133.

6

Articulation

Just as tempo and dynamics are often not indicated in baroque music, articulation marks may be absent as well. Choosing an appropriate bow stroke or tonguing to achieve the desired articulation nevertheless constitutes an essential part of playing in style and of correct expression. Quantz describes the choice of appropriate articulation as a process of giving "life" to the notes; the performer thus has the ability to add life (character or spirit) to the music through the attack, bowing, or tonguing chosen for each note. While performing as a soloist, one has considerable freedom in the use of articulation, but in a group the articulation must be chosen carefully so that each part contributes its share to the spirit of the music. Quantz's description of its expressive uses demonstrates that a given passage may suggest a variety of articulations; the performer's role is to choose the one most appropriate:

In the performance of music on the violin and the instruments similar to it the bow stroke is of chief importance. Through it the sound is drawn from the instrument well or poorly, the notes receive their life, the Piano and Forte are expressed, the passions are aroused, and the melancholy is distinguished from the gay, the serious from the jocular, the sublime from the flattering, the modest from the bold. In a word, like the chest, tongue, and lips on the flute, the bow-stroke provides the means for achieving musical articulation, and for varying a single idea in diverse ways. That the fingers must also contribute their share, and that you must have a good instrument and true strings, is self-evident, But since, even with all of these things, the execution may still be very defective, no matter how accurately and truly you stop the strings, how well the instrument sounds, or how good the strings are, it follows that, with regard to execution, the bow-stroke is of central importance.

I will illustrate what I have said with an example. Play the passage [below] in a moderate tempo entirely with long strokes of the full bow.

Afterwards diminish the length of the strokes, and play the same notes several times with successively shorter strokes. Then one time give a stress to each stroke with the bow, another time play the example *staccato*, that is, with all the strokes detached. Although each note will have received its separate stroke, the expression will be different each time. The expression will be equally varied if you try the example with different kinds of slurs, and play the sixteenth notes with one stroke, then as if dots beneath a slur appear above the notes, then two notes with one stroke, then one staccato and three slurred, or the first detached and the remaining notes slurred with single strokes for each pair.

This example is sufficient proof of the harm that incorrect use of the bow can do, and of the varied effects that its correct handling can produce. It follows that in a ripieno part neither the violinist nor any other performer upon a bowed instrument has the freedom to slur or detach the notes as he pleases; he is obliged to play them with the bowing the composer has indicated at those places which deviate from the customary manner.[1]

Quantz's description of different types of bow strokes is important for several reasons: (1) it demonstrates that the eighteenth-century violinist could choose from among a variety of legato, staccato, and slurred strokes, (2) it emphasizes the principle that in orchestral playing a violinist must use the same articulations as others in the ensemble, and (3) it confirms that a player must follow the bowings indicated by the composer, for the articulations indicated in the score may be those that "deviate from the customary manner." Thus, many articulations, particularly those that indicate the usual or customary manner, may not be marked at all. They must be added by the performer in accordance with the style and character of the piece.

For an understanding of the expressive use of articulation during the baroque era, it is helpful to explore the relationships between different types of articulation used by singers and players of string, wind, and keyboard instruments. Although there are some fundamental differences in the way articulations are executed on different instruments, their effects are often similar.

In performing baroque chamber music, there are many opportunities for singers and instrumentalists to match their articulations to one another. An imitative passage, for example, may require similar articulations from different instruments, or two or more continuo players may double the bass line and therefore may be obliged to use similar articulations. Woodwinds, too, frequently double the violins in ensemble music and must match their articulations to those of the strings. Players may arrive at the same articulation by different technical means, but they must begin by formulating a similar concept of the desired sound.

Various sources and documents can lead us to a better understanding of baroque articulations. Of prime importance are the many treatises on individual instruments and their playing techniques. They provide specific information both about an individual composer's practice and about the customary manners of performance in a particular place. By comparing several treatises, we are able to gain some knowledge of techniques that were practiced over a certain period or a larger geographical area. Naturally the effect of a particular articulation can be varied according to the player's wishes and is subject to one's skill and ability to control the instrument. Some treatises, such as those by Muffat (1698) and Quantz (1752), are concerned specifically with orchestral playing; others by Corrette and Geminiani deal primarily with solo playing. The following discussion provides a few examples of some articulation practices that were widely known during the baroque era.

Lully and seventeenth-century French orchestral practice

One of the earliest discussions of articulation is Georg Muffat's preface to *Florilegium secundum* (1698),[2] in which the author attempts to describe the style of orchestral bowing prevalent in France during the last quarter of the seventeenth century. That the style he describes was also practiced outside of France as well is apparent from his observation that the manner of bowing under Lully has already been accepted by the "French, English, and those from the Low Countries," and he argues for its acceptance in Germany. It is important to note that his rules apply to orchestral playing, and that he stresses the importance of a unified style of articulation, "even if a thousand play." The articulation ought to be stronger, according to Muffat, in orchestral performance than it is in solo playing.

Although his discussion is concerned mainly with violin playing, similar principles can be applied to woodwinds, since the oboes often doubled the violins in orchestral music, and bassoons also doubled the basso continuo. When reading Muffat's comments, we must also keep in mind that the bows used by French orchestral players at the end of the seventeenth century were shorter than those used for sonatas and solo playing, and they were held using a thumb-under grip, with the player's thumb pressing upward on the hair (see Figure 3). The short bow allowed the player to lift and retake the bow stroke with ease (by using successive downbows) and favored short, fairly strong strokes.

Figure 3. Gerrit Dou (1613–1675), *Geigespieler* [Violin Player].

According to Muffat, the first basic principle of orchestral playing in the French style is that all important notes must be played with a down stroke.[3] His examples show that "good" notes are those that receive strong metrical accents: the first and third beats in Common time, or the first beat in triple meter. The "good" notes, also called *noble* or *principal*, are therefore played with stress and a downbow stroke. Muffat marks these notes "n" for *nobilis* [good], and the metrically weak ones "v" for *vilis* [poor].[4] He uses the symbols ⌐ or *n* to show a downbow stroke and *v* or · for an upbow. Two of his symbols bear an obvious similarity to those still used today for downbow and upbow strokes (⌐ and ∨), although it is not known whether they originate with Muffat. In order to maintain the principle of downbow strokes on first beats in a triple meter (or other meters with an odd number of beats per measure), it is necessary to retake the bow at the beginning of each measure, or in more lively tempos to play two notes on the same upbow stroke in a detached manner, which he calls *craquer*. The resulting articulations produce a strongly accented, separate articulation, without the addition of any slurs, and with a silence of articulation created by lifting the bow before the downbeat (see Example 6-1a, c). When there is time, downbow strokes are even retaken within a measure, as shown in Example 6-1b (m. 3, beats 3 and 4). He observes that members of Lully's orchestra "all observe the same way of playing the principal notes in the measure: above all, those that begin the measure, those that define the cadence, and those that most clearly emphasize the dance rhythm."[5] Muffat's examples of bowings in different meters show that some liberty was allowed in fast dances, such as gigues and bourrées, where the upbow stroke may be detached (not slurred, however) when there is no time for retaking the bow (Example 6-2a, b).

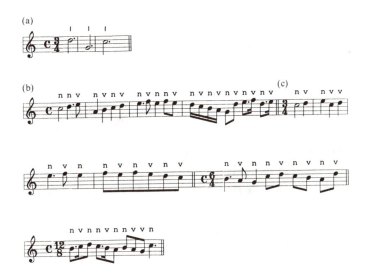

Example 6-1a, b, c. Georg Muffat, Retaking the bow in the French style, from *Florilegium secundum*, 1698.

Example 6-2a, b. Muffat, The detached bow stroke, from *Florilegium secundum*, 1698.

Muffat also describes the way of playing successive notes which, though notated equally, are performed unequally by lengthening the first note of each pair. This manner of interpretation, called *inégalité*, or *notes inégales*, was also described by Saint-Lambert, François Couperin, and Michel Corrette (see chapter 7). The lengthening of the first note incorporated a gentle, or sometimes even a pronounced, stress, and it may therefore be considered a type of articulation. Muffat's description of the practice shows that it was used predominantly for the smallest note value in a given meter, and ordinarily in stepwise motion, in either quick or slow tempos.

> Diminutions of the first order such as sixteenth notes in four-beat measures, eighth notes in 2 or *alla breve* measures, or notes that last a half-beat in slightly quick triple meters and their proportions are, when used successively, not played each equal to the next, as they are written: for that would make them somewhat boring, crude, and dull. But they are altered in the French style, by lengthening each odd-numbered note the value of a dot, making the following note shorter by the same amount. Observe the different types, in different meters [Example 6-3a]; note also in which way they should be played, when the occasion permits it [Example 6-3b].[6]

Muffat does not mention the addition of slurs when performing *notes inégales*. In order to retain the variety of articulation on individual notes that he advises, it is usually preferable to use single bow or tongue strokes when adding inequality, at least in orchestral playing.

An instrumental piece that may be studied in conjunction with Muffat's principles of articulation is the French ouverture. Inaugurated by Lully as a piece to precede the prologue of an opera or ballet, its formal characteristics became standardized after a period of some experimentation (see the ouverture to Lully's *Le bourgeois gentilhomme* [1670], Appendix A). In 1700, Freillon-Poncein describes the ouverture as a piece that begins with a section that is "either serious [*grave*] or light [*léger*] in duple meter," which is followed by a second section, either slow or quick, in another meter. If the second part is quick, it should

Example 6-3a, b. Rhythmic inequality in the French style, according to Muffat.

conclude with "several measures" of a slower pace.[7] Lully's ouvertures frequently consist of two sections: a noble or grand opening in duple meter played by the entire orchestra, followed by a faster, often imitative, section, usually in a different meter, which may feature woodwind trios and other textural changes. Some of his ouvertures (especially those written after 1673) also have a shorter third section featuring a return to the original tempo. Although Muffat does not mention the French ouverture by name, he includes pieces with that title in the suites of his *Florilegium primum* (1695), and his rules of articulation may appropriately be applied to such pieces. He describes a type of sharp dotting of notes, usually called "overdotting" or "double dotting" today, which should be observed particularly in pieces whose tempo is moderate or slow. This would be appropriate in the opening section of the French ouverture (see "overdotting" in chapter 7). The short, faster notes preceding the accented first beat were performed with separate strokes of the bow, arriving on a down-bow at the beginning of each measure. According to Muffat, "the little (pickup) note by itself before the beginning of the measure as well as the one that passes quickly after a dot or after a short rest . . . should always be up-bow." Examples of the French ouverture can be found in France for at least half a century after Lully's death by composers such as Campra, Leclair, and Rameau, and the style was also imitated by composers outside of France such as Handel and Bach.

The emergence of solo styles of articulation in the eighteenth century

The individuality inherent in solo performance allowed a greater variety of articulation, including combinations of slurred and separate notes. Although slurs were known to players in the seventeenth century, it appears that they were marked only infrequently, especially in printed sources. One might, however, add a few when they enhance the spirit of the movement.

In seventeenth-century chamber music for violins or viols, occasional slurs can be found, although they are quite rare. In Biber's Sonata No. 9 for two violins, three violas, and continuo from *Sonatae tam aris quam aulis servientes* (1676),[8] for example, slurs occur in arpeggio-like figuration for the violins (Example 6-4). In a section marked *adagio,* four repeated notes are marked with a tie and dots to indicate a detached bow stroke in all the parts. When the same indication occurs over many repeated notes, the effect may be either a rapid or slow tremolo performed in one bow stroke, sometimes also called bow vibrato.[9]

Example 6-4. Biber, Sonata No. 9 from *Sonatae tam aris quam aulis servientes* (1676), with slurs and articulation marks.

Buxtehude also indicates slurs occasionally in his sonatas for violin, viola da gamba, and harpsichord, which were published in two collections (*VII Sonate à doi* [sic], Op. 1, Hamburg, 1694; *VII Suonate à due*, Op. 2, Hamburg, 1696).[10] The presence of such marks in the works of Biber, Buxtehude, and others suggests that in passages where no slurs are indicated, the convention was to play mostly with separate strokes. Other possibilities to consider are whether slurs might belong to the character of certain dance pieces, and whether manuscript and printed sources of a work might show different marks. In seventeenth-century music, it is preferable to add only those slurs that enhance the affect or spirit of the piece.

An early eighteenth-century example of the use of varied articulation in French music for solo viol is Marin Marais's *Pièces de viole* (Book 2, 1701).[11] In his preface, Marais explains the meaning of dots marked under a slur as a "single bow stroke in which several notes are articulated as if they were done by different bow strokes, by pressing a little on the finger that touches the hair of the bow." Marais assumes that the player is using the palm-up grip of the bow in which the middle finger touches the hair. This grip and additional articulation with the middle finger produced a strong upbow stroke and also allowed more than one articulation within a single bow stroke. He uses dots to warn the player "that each note must be played equally, in the places where one would ordinarily dot (i.e., lengthen) the first note." In this case, dots indicate the absence of *notes inégales* and should not be confused with staccato marks.

In addition to indicating precise bowings in his music, Marais includes signs for two types of vibrato, fingerings, and several types of ornaments (for a fuller explanation of the latter, see chapter 8). A "Fantaisie" from his *Pièces de violes* (Book 3, 1711) includes two extraordinarily long slurs indicating single bow strokes, one with vibrato (♮) and a swell (*e*) in mm. 26–28, and another over thirty-six notes on a downbow stroke (marked *t* for *tirer*; mm. 29–31). Other notes in this piece are played with separate strokes, and a quick tempo can be inferred from the presence of the two long slurs. In addition to fingerings, Marais also indicates the mordent (x) and trill (𝄐). The mark (••) indicates that a note is to be played on the second string in m. 14 (Example 6-5). The numbers indicate fingerings, with 0 representing an open string.

In his method for violin of 1738 entitled *L'école d'Orphée*, Michel Corrette also provides an example of the judicious use of slurs to enhance expression in solo playing. His description of how to play a sarabande (Example 6-6) is particularly instructive because it includes dynamics (crescendo and diminuendo) and bowings. These marks suggest how a soloist might interpret the piece, but the articulation marks themselves are more reminiscent of orchestral playing, with downbow strokes on strong beats and some retaking of the bow.

Example 6-5. Marin Marais, "Fantaisie" from *3ᵉ livre de pièces de violes* (Paris, 1711).

In sarabandes, adagios, largos, and other expressive pieces, it is necessary to play the whole notes, half notes, and quarter notes with long bow strokes and swell the sounds at the end (A, B). But for the ends of phrases and of sections, it is necessary to begin the bow stroke quietly, strengthen it in the middle, and finish it by diminishing the sound (C, D, E). This bow stroke makes a very beautiful effect.

Example 6-6. Corrette, Sarabande for violin with articulation and dynamic marks, from *L'école d'Orphée* (Paris, 1738).

Late baroque solo and orchestral playing

The principles of bowing described by Muffat remained in use well into the eighteenth century, both in France and elsewhere in Europe. Orchestral playing in general relied upon clean, crisp articulations, and the French and Italian styles of bowing, as described by Corrette (*L'école d'Orphée*, 1738), retain the separate strokes characteristic of earlier practice. They differ principally in the greater use in the French style of the downbow-on-the-downbeat rule described by Muffat. Those in the Italian style make use of alternate strokes, generally without retaking the bow.

When French music was performed outside of France, we can assume that the playing style described by Muffat was also practiced. Whenever composers imitated the French style in their music, it is also appropriate to consider performing according to French ideas of articulation and spirit. Thus, French dances and ouvertures in the operas and oratorios of Handel and the suites of Bach would seem to lie directly within the tradition of orchestral playing described by Muffat and still practiced in France well into the eighteenth century.

In the eighteenth century, we find less evidence of a strong distinction between articulation in orchestral and solo playing. Ensemble playing, however, continued to require the use of separate notes and an attempt, whenever possible, to arrive at a downbow stroke at the beginning of each measure. Much eighteenth-century ensemble music contains few slurs at all, and those that are present fall most often in pairs, or more rarely, on three or four notes. In the first movement of Bach's *Orchestral Suite (Ouverture) No. 1 in C* (BWV 1066),[12] the violin part contains passages in tutti sections without any slurs, as well as passages for the solo violin in which Bach calls for a greater variety of articulations. The principal aim of ensemble playing remained the precision of articulation, in which players matched their own strokes to those of the leader and were not free to add their own slurs.

Robert Bremner, who was a pupil of Geminiani, provided some observations on both solo and orchestral playing. In his preface to J. G. C. Schetky's *Six Quartettos for Two Violins, a Tenor, & Violoncello... Op. VI* (London, 1777),[13] Bremner recommends use of little vibrato, applying it only occasionally on long notes "for the sake of variety." His remarks stress the importance of uniformity of expression and articulation that remained a part of both orchestral and choral performance even after 1750:

From what has been observed above, it must follow, that when gentlemen are performing in concert, should they, instead of considering themselves as relative parts of one great whole, assume each of them the discretional power of applying tremolos, shakes, beats, appogiaturas, together with some of them slurring, while others are articulating, the same notes; or, in other words, carrying all their different solo-playing powers into an orchestral performance; a concert thus rebellious cannot be productive of any noble effect.*

*Choruses, the most awful [i.e., awe-inspiring] of all music entertainments, are too often performed in this undisciplined manner; not intentionally, but from ill-judged ambition, which fires the breasts of many singers with a desire of excelling their neighbours in skill and vociferation. Should he who hath thus transgressed, make it his future study to render his performance useful rather than conspicuous; and at the same time not strain beyond the natural strength of voice which affords pleasure, public complaint will give place to public admiration.[14]

On the proper manner of bowing, he suggests consulting Tartini's *Letter* (discussed below in this section) and equates the bowing techniques of solo and orchestral playing, recommending always that the music be performed exactly as it is marked. Given the significance that eighteenth-century authors attached to the bow stroke on the violin, it will be useful to examine several sources by Geminiani, Tartini, and Leopold Mozart that discuss articulation in some detail.

In his *Art of Playing on the Violin* (London, 1751), Geminiani includes a valuable table of articulations proper to the violin, in which he illustrates the manner of adding articulation when it is not indicated, including slurs, staccato, and even dynamic nuances. He does not attempt to formulate rules of bowing, but rather to indicate how the melody and rhythm provide clues to the appropriate articulation. He provides examples of passages marked "good," "bad," and "unusual" [*particolare*, for a special effect], as shown in Table 6-1. In some of his studies for the violin, Geminiani uses the same marks to indicate correct articulations. He also describes the use of the *messa di voce* on long notes in solo playing:

One of the principal Beauties of the Violin is the swelling or encreasing (sic) and softening the Sound; which is done by pressing the Bow upon the Strings with the Fore-finger more or less. In playing all long Notes the Sound should be begun soft, and gradually swelled till the Middle, and from thence gradually softened till the End.[15]

Geminiani's principles may be applied to most solo music in the Italian style belonging to the first half of the eighteenth century. In J. S. Bach's music, few slurs need to be added, for they are usually indicated, but in much of Handel's and Telemann's music, there are few marks written in, and the player is obliged to add slurs and articulations that suit the tempo and character of the piece.

Tartini's advice for articulation on the violin can be studied in a letter written in Padua and dated March 5, 1760, addressed to a certain pupil, Signora Maddalena Lombardini. Charles Burney translated the letter into English, publishing it in 1779 as an "important lesson to performers on the violin." Tartini attaches importance to the swell on long notes and recommends practicing it at an early stage. He first advises his pupil to practice diligently the swell on an open string, in which "you begin *pianissimo*, and increase the tone by slow degrees to its *fortissimo* (Tartini, 13)." Eventually one should add both a crescendo and diminuendo in the same stroke, "beginning with the most minute softness, increasing the tone to its loudest degree, and diminishing it to the same point of softness with which you began, and all this in the same stroke of the bow." For the

Table 6-1. Articulations used in violin playing, from Geminiani's *Art of Playing the Violin* (London, 1751).

"light pulsation and play of the wrist" he recommends practicing passages in sixteenth notes, playing the notes "*staccato*, that is, separated and detached, with a little space between every two, for though they are written thus:

they should be played as if there was a rest after every note, in this manner (Tartini, 15):"

Leopold Mozart in 1756 devotes considerable space to the bow stroke and articulation on the violin. His words are reminiscent of Quantz's:

> the bowing gives life to the notes; . . . it produces now a modest, now an impertinent, now a serious or playful tone; now coaxing, or grave and sublime; now a sad or merry melody; and is therefore the medium by the reasonable use of which we are able to rouse in the hearers the aforesaid affects.[16]

Woodwind articulation

Articulation for the woodwind player consists of the use of syllables in tonguing that produce a softer or louder attack. French players used short syllables whose consonants were either hard or soft, such as *tu* and *ru*, and alternated them in a manner that produced a slightly uneven rhythm, called inequality or *notes inégales*. Though notated equally, certain notes—usually the shorter note values in a piece—were played with inequality in a pattern of long-short rhythms that could vary from barely perceptible to very dotted depending upon the tempo and character of the piece.

Hotteterre, in *Principes de la flûte traversière, de la flûte à bec, et du hautbois* of 1707, recommended the use of these two alternating syllables "to render playing more agreeable and to avoid too much uniformity in the tongue strokes."[17] The more common stroke is *tu*, which is used on whole and half notes, quarter notes, and on most eighth notes, either on a repeated pitch or on a leap. In passages that are diatonic, he suggests alternating *tu* with *ru* as a general rule. Sometimes the decision as to whether to use *tu* exclusively or to alternate *tu* and *ru* depends upon the meter. In the following example (Example 6-7), the meters suggest a fast, detached manner of playing that requires the use of *tu* except on weak notes

Example 6-7. The use of *tu* and *ru* in tonguing, as shown in Hotteterre's *Principes de la flûte traversière, de la flûte à bec, et du hautbois* (1707).

within the sixteenth-note groups. The alternation of *tu* and *ru* in eighth-note passages produces a softly slurred articulation and is appropriate for passages requiring inequality, according to Hotteterre:

> One will do well to observe that one must not always play eighth notes equally, but that one must, in certain meters, make one of them long and one short, which is also ruled by their number. When the number is even, one makes the first one long, the second one short, and so on for the others. When it is odd, one does the contrary: that is called "pointing" [*pointer*]. The meters in which this is most ordinarily practiced are those in 2, 3, and 6/4 [Example 6-7].[18]

Noting the differences between woodwind instruments in the attack of tongue strokes, he recommends that tonguings "be more or less articulated, according to the instrument one plays; for example, one softens them on the transverse flute. One marks them more on the recorder, and one pronounces them much more strongly on the oboe (Hotteterre, 27)." The slurred articulation, consisting of several notes played with the same tonguing, he calls the *coulez*. Two or more notes may be slurred with the *tu* stroke (Example 6-8).

Example 6-8. The *coulez*, or slurred tonguing, according to Hotteterre's *Principes de la flûte traversière, de la flûte à bec, et du hautbois* (1707).

Hotteterre's *Principes* continued to be printed until 1765, and there is considerable evidence that the type of tonguing he describes remained in common use. Instructions for playing the flute in Peter Prelleur's *The Modern Musik-Master or, the Universal Musician*, published in London in 1731, follow Hotteterre's principles closely, using the same syllables, *tu* and *ru*. Quantz (1752) also favored alternating syllables, such as *ti-tiri* and *di-diri*. These articulations were also used by flute, oboe, and bassoon players, as well as by recorder players. For Corrette in 1735 and Mahaut in 1759, the tongue strokes were not to be limited to *tu* and *ru*, for slurs of more than two notes were more frequent in later music, as well as detached notes. The slurred articulation, called *lourer*, required a tonguing so soft that the articulation was scarcely noticeable.

Quantz also describes double tonguing, in which two syllables ("did'll") are employed for "the very quickest passage-work (Quantz, 79)." The use of *did'll* produces a slight metric accent on each beat or "good" note, whereas the two syllables *tiri*, he says, give an accent to the second syllable.

Articulation in singing

Because of the words a singer pronounces, articulation is often more apparent in the vocal part and may serve as a model to players in an ensemble. Although the writers of vocal treatises did not usually discuss articulation as thoroughly as those who wrote instrumental treatises did, they do suggest a few general rules that may provide the basis for understanding the clarity of articulation demanded by baroque music.

Tosi offers an explanation of articulations for the singer that correspond to the violinist's separate and slurred bow strokes. He recognizes two types of division (that is, passage work) for the voice, one called "mark'd" and another called "gliding." The first, equivalent to separate bow strokes, is a "light Motion of the Voice, in which the Notes that constitute the Division be all articulate in equal Proportion, and moderately distinct, that they be not too much join'd, nor too much mark'd (Tosi, 52)." This articulation is more frequently used, according to Tosi, and is "something like the *Staccato* on the violin, but not too much." The "gliding," or slurred type of articulation, is "performed in such a Manner that the first Note is a Guide to all that follow, closely united, gradual, and with such Evenness of Motion, that in Singing it imitates a certain Gliding, by the Masters called a *Slur*; the effect of which is truly agreeable when used sparingly (Tosi, 53)." He recommends limiting the use of the slur in singing to a few notes, either ascending, or especially in descending. He adds that such use of a slur "cannot go beyond a fourth without displeasing." These *"Gliding Notes* are like several Notes in one stroke of the Bow on the Violin." The two kinds of *division*, according to Tosi, should be mixed within phrases according to the musical and textual demands. He also describes another type of slurred articulation called the *"Dragg,* [which] consists in a Succession of divers Notes, artfully mixed with the *Forte* and *Piano*." He does not elaborate upon how the *Dragg* may be used, but it probably represents a slur in which nuanced dynamics are added for expressive value. In much baroque music, the slurs implied by the text underlay often provide clues for appropriate articulations when accompanying the voice, since articulations are more frequently indicated in the vocal part than in the basso continuo or obbligato (solo) instrument.

Keyboard articulation

Articulation on the harpsichord is affected only to a limited extent by the speed of attack, since its action consists of a plucking rather than a striking of the strings. Other factors that affect articulation, especially in continuo playing, are the speed of arpeggiation and the texture of the part. A chord of many notes that is played with little or no arpeggiation will sound louder and more accented than one of fewer notes which is spread more slowly. On both the organ and harpsichord, a small silence of articulation before a note or chord also produces an accent. Early fingerings are a good source of clues about articulation on keyboard instruments and may allow some pieces to be played more easily.

Sources for the study of fingering practices in baroque music are of two types: (1) instruction books that comment upon the player's posture and touch and include fingered scales or exercises, and (2) fingerings marked in manuscripts and other musical sources. Numerous systems of fingering were used at different times and places during the baroque era.

An important Italian source for the early baroque is Girolamo Diruta's *Il transilvano* (1593; part 2, 1609), the first treatise to distinguish between different touches and styles of playing on the harpsichord and organ. On the organ, according to Diruta, one should connect harmonies smoothly using a legato touch; lifting the hands to strike the keys is permissible only when playing dances [*balli*]. The harpsichord, with its quilled action, allows a leaping style of playing, and the player is advised to ornament while playing in order to have a full sound. His system of fingering relates "good" fingers (2 and 4 of each hand) to "good" notes, usually those that are consonant and fall on downbeats. A good finger usually alternates with a "bad" one in patterns such as 2–3–2–3 or 4–3–4–3, and the thumb is not used on black notes.

Early seventeenth-century fingering practice in England can be studied in numerous pieces for virginal that survive in manuscript copies. Most of the fingerings follow the principle of good and bad notes outlined by Diruta, except that in England, the third finger was used as a strong finger in both hands, and the thumb was also considered a strong finger. In some passages, all five fingers were used, and there are also fingerings which show the thumb passing under other fingers.

Evidence of a transition between the concept of good and bad notes to one in which fingers are used on a more-or-less equal basis can be seen in J. S. Bach's music. A short example, or *applicatio*, for Wilhelm Friedemann Bach is fingered according to the practice of the English virginalists, with the third finger falling on good notes as in m. 1 (Example 6-9) and the thumb used as a strong finger in alternation with the second finger (m. 3). Fingerings in J. S. Bach's C major prelude (BWV 870a), an early version of that in Book 2 of the *Well-Tempered Clavier*, show that paired fingerings were rarely used in more complex passages (Example 6-10).[19]

Example 6-9. J. S. Bach, *Applicatio* from the notebook for Wilhelm Friedemann Bach, with original fingerings.

In a few places the left-hand pattern 2–1–2–1 appears in stepwise motion (for example, mm. 5 and 10). Common fingerings in other German sources during the first half of the eighteenth century include patterns such as 3–4–3–4–3–4–3 (right hand ascending) and 3–2–1–2–1–2–1–2 (left hand ascending) starting at c^1; descending patterns starting at c^1 were 5–4–3–2–3–2–3, ending 1 (right hand), and 2–3–2–3–2–3–2, ending 4 (left hand).[20]

Another practice can be observed in François Couperin's *L'art de toucher le clavecin* (1716), in which strong notes are not necessarily taken with strong fingers. In scale passages, the longer third finger may be passed over the fourth when ascending, and the third over the second finger when descending. The resulting patterns are 3–4–3–4 ascending and 3–2–3–2 descending, or when accidentals are involved, 2–3–4–2–3–4 and 4–3–2–4–3–2 (Example 6-11).

Couperin also includes an extended discussion of articulation, touch, and ornamentation on the harpsichord. In the following passage, he describes the effect of allowing two or more simultaneous notes to be played with a slight delay between them. He likens the effect to the *messa di voce* on string instruments and considers this type of delay or arpeggiation the key to expressive playing on the harpsichord:

The feeling or "soul," the expressive effect, which I mean, is due to the *cessation* and *suspension* of the notes, made at the right moment,

Example 6-10. J. S. Bach, C major prelude (BWV 870a), with fingerings preserved in a manuscript copied by J. C. Vogler.

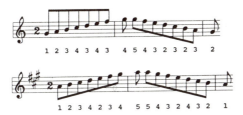

Example 6-11. Fingering of scale passages from François Couperin's *L'art de toucher le clavecin* (Paris, 1716).

and in accordance with the character required by the melodies of the Preludes and Pieces. These two *agréments*, by their contrast, leave the ear in suspense, so that in such cases where string instruments would increase their volume of sound, the *suspension* (slight retardation) of the sounds on the Harpsichord seems (by a contrary effect) to produce on the ear the result expected and desired.

In succeeding paragraphs, he emphasizes the importance of legato when playing the harpsichord, accomplished by holding down notes and by changing fingers on a note in order to keep it sounding. He provides several examples from his own music to illustrate these principles. In "La Milordine," from his *Ier livre de pièces de clavecin* (Paris, 1713), he suggests changing fingers while holding tied notes for a legato phrasing.

Summary: Choosing an articulation

Articulation in singing and playing consists of slurred and separate notes produced by pronunciation, tonguing, bowing, or touch. In the baroque era, articulation was believed to add "life" to the notes and to contribute substantially to the music's spirit. Most articulations were varied according to the note's metrical placement (stronger on "good" beats) and the melodic shape of a phrase (with a stress on the highest note, for example). Orchestral playing, represented by Lully's practices as described by Muffat, required precision and knowledge of the downbow-on-the-downbeat principle, whereas solo playing allowed the performer more freedom to add slurs and a variety of different articulations. Along with nuanced dynamics and ornamentation, articulation was an important part of playing in style, and a knowledge of the variety of articulations available to the player will lend an agreeable variety and interest to modern performances of baroque music.

Bibliographical notes

Most specific information about articulation comes from treatises on individual instruments (for a list of pre-1800 sources cited in this book, see Appendix C). A composer's preface to a collection of music may also be useful for questions concerning articulation. Among modern sources, Howard Ferguson's book on keyboard playing is informative and filled with musical observations. Numerous systems of keyboard fingering were practiced during the baroque era at different times and places, and the extent to which they affected the music is not fully known. An informative summary is presented by Peter Le Hurray in "Fingering [before 1750]" in *Grove*, and by Mark Lindley in *Performance Practice: Music after 1600*. Lindley's "Early Fingering: Some Editing Problems . . ." outlines difficulties players (and editors) encounter in working with manuscripts, and he identifies errors in numerous modern editions.

FOR FURTHER STUDY

Boxall, Maria, ed. *Harpsichord Studies: Thirteen Preludes and Voluntaries with Original Fingerings from R.C.M. Ms. 2093 and B.L. Add. Ms. 31403*. London: Schott, 1980.

Butt, John. *Bach Interpretation: Articulation Marks in Primary Sources of J. S. Bach*. Cambridge: Cambridge University Press, 1990.

Cooper, Kenneth, and Julius Zsako, transl. "Georg Muffat's Observations on the Lully Style of Performance." *MQ* 53 (1967): 220–245.

Faulkner, Quentin. *J. S. Bach's Keyboard Technique: a Historical Introduction*. St. Louis: Concordia Publishing House, 1984.

Ferguson, Howard. *Keyboard Interpretation from the Fourteenth to the Nineteenth Century, an Introduction*. London: Oxford University Press, 1975.

Hammond, Frederick. "The Performance of Frescobaldi's Keyboard Music." In *Girolamo Frescobaldi*, 222–251. Cambridge: Harvard University Press, 1983.

Hsu, John. *A Handbook of French Baroque Viol Technique*. New York: Broude Brothers Limited, 1981.

Kolneder, Walter. *Georg Muffat zur Aufführungspraxis*. Strasbourg: P. H. Heitz, 1970.

Lindley, Mark. "Early Fingering: Some Editing Problems and Some New Readings for J. S. Bach and John Bull." *EM* 17 (February 1989), 60–69.

_____. "Keyboard Fingerings and Articulations." In *Performance Practice: Music after 1600*, 86–203. Ed. Howard Mayer Brown and Stanley Sadie. New York: W. W. Norton & Co., 1989.

_____. "Keyboard Technique and Articulation: Evidence for the Performance Practices of Bach, Handel, and Scarlatti." In *Bach, Handel, Scarlatti: Tercentenary Essays*. Ed. Peter Williams, 207–243. Cambridge: Cambridge University Press, 1985.

Powell, Newman Wilson. "Early Keyboard Fingering and its Effect upon Articulation." *JAMS* 6 (1953): 252–253.

NOTES TO CHAPTER 6

1. *Quantz*, 215–217.
2. In Kolneder (in the four original languages: French, German, Latin, and Italian), 39–101; see also the English translation in the article by Cooper and Zsako. Both are listed in the bibliography at the end of this chapter. Muffat's *Florilegium primum* and *Florilegium secundum* are in *DTÖ*, v. 2 (Jahrgang 1:2) and v. 4 (Jahrgang 1:2); both ed. Heinrich Rietsch (Graz: Akademische Druck-u. Verlagsanstalt, 1959).
3. Kolneder, 57f.
4. Kolneder, 83 and ex. Oo (sic).
5. Kolneder, 57f.
6. Kolneder, 73.
7. Freillon-Poncein, 54.
8. *DTÖ*, v. 106–107, ed. Erich Schenk (Graz: Akademische Druck-u. Verlagsanstalt, 1963), 98–112.
9. See Stewart Carter, "The String Tremolo in the 17th Century," *EM* 19 (February 1991), 43–59.
10. *DDT*, ser. 1, v. 11, ed. Carl Stiehl, rev. Hans Joachim Moser (Wiesbaden: Breitkopf & Härtel, 1957).
11. Marin Marais, *Pièces de viole, 2ᵉ livre*, ed. John Hsu (New York: Broude Trust, 1986), facs. of preface, p. 250f and English transl., 251–253.
12. *NBA*, series 7, v. 1, ed. Heinrich Besseler (Kassel: Bärenreiter, 1967).

13. See Bremner's preface and a detailed commentary in Neal Zaslaw, "The Complete Orchestral Musician," *EM* 7 (January 1979), 46–57.
14. Zaslaw, 52.
15. Geminiani, *The Art of Playing on the Violin,* ed. Boyden, 2.
16. L. Mozart, *A Treatise on the Fundamental Principles of Violin Playing,* transl. Knocker, 114.
17. Hotteterre, *Principes,* facs. reprint of the Amsterdam, 1728 ed. (Kassel: Bärenreiter-Verlag, 1958), 21. Translations are mine.
18. Hotteterre, p. 22.
19. A facsimile of the manuscript (P. 1089 folio 4v) is in James A. Brokaw II, "The Genesis of the Prelude in C Major, BWV 870," *Bach Studies,* ed. Don O. Franklin (Cambridge: Cambridge University Press, 1989), 225–239.
20. For further examples and theoretical evidence from Germany, see Quentin Falkner, *J. S. Bach's Keyboard Technique: a Historical Introduction* (St. Louis: Concordia Publishing House, 1984).

7

Rhythm and Notation

We have seen that many aspects of performance were taken for granted in baroque music, either because the composer left the choice to the performer, or because conventions of notation were widely known at the time. In addition, some characteristics that belong to the style of performing cannot be rendered precisely in musical notation. When a tradition depends heavily upon established convention, improvisation, or oral transmission, the notation may represent only a skeleton or framework of the music, which is virtually recreated each time it is performed. Two examples of schematic notation that were not performed as written are the unmeasured prelude and recitative.

Among the most prevalent notational conventions in the baroque era are those associated with rhythm, for composers intentionally wrote inexact rhythms in many circumstances. Although the notation probably created little problem for the baroque performer, it is often a cause for confusion today. French music in particular was subject to two types of rhythmic alteration, either overdotting (also called double dotting) in the ouverture, courante, and certain other movements, or inequality (playing notes unequally that are notated equally). A third type of rhythmic alteration that was understood in the baroque era—and even well into the nineteenth century—was the rhythmic alignment of dotted notes and triplets.

The unmeasured prelude

A short, improvised prelude often used to test the tuning of a keyboard or fretted instrument became popular in France during the early seventeenth century. First performed by lutenists, such pieces from about the middle of the century onward were composed for the harpsichord and written down, primarily in manuscripts of harpsichord music by Louis Couperin, Nicolas Lebègue (1631–1702), and Jean-Baptiste-Henri d'Anglebert. The unusual notation employed for the prelude was intended to retain as much of its improvisatory character as possible by leaving the rhythm almost entirely to the performer. Called *préludes non mesurés* (unmeasured, or free preludes), these works belong largely to the seventeenth century, although there are a few later examples, including one by Rameau (1706[1]) and another by Claude Balbastre written about 1770,[2] which may have been intended for the pianoforte. Thus the tradition of recreating an improvisation from the schematic notation of the unmeasured prelude existed for well over a century in France. The style was occasionally imitated outside of France as well, as can be seen in the Prelude in A major for harpsichord by Handel.

Most of the surviving unmeasured preludes are by Louis Couperin and d'Anglebert. When they are performed, one hears a progression of chords arpeggiated freely in different ways, with ornamentation such as trills and passing notes. Some more extended preludes often include a more rhythmically measured, usually imitative, section, and conclude with a return to the free, chordal texture at the end. At first glance the notation bears little resemblance to the sound in performance, because many of the preludes are written entirely in whole notes (especially those of Louis Couperin), or in a combination of whole notes and a few smaller note values (as in those of Lebègue, d'Anglebert, and Rameau). Chords can be recognized not by vertical position but rather by the slurs (called *tenües*) that graphically illustrate the harmonic motion and tell the performer which notes are to be held down. It is left to the performer to determine the speed and to distinguish between harmony and melody (see the Prelude in F by Louis Couperin in Appendix A).

Most clues about how to play these preludes come from the music itself, but a few other hints have also been uncovered. The composer DeMachy left a useful preface (*avertissement*) to his *Pièces de violle* (Book I, 1685) in which he directs that the unmeasured preludes for viol may be played "as one wishes, either fast or slow."[3] The only document that preserves directions for performing them on the harpsichord is an autograph letter from Lebègue to an Englishman, which is preserved in a copy of the 1677 print of Lebègue's music at Yale University.[4] It contains three points of considerable interest in regard to performing unmeasured preludes: (1) the slurs found on both chord tones and passing notes (nonchord tones) indicate written-out arpeggios; (2) notes may be sustained in one part while another part is moving—over a pedal, for example—and a sustained chord may be restruck; (3) barlines and oblique lines are a visual indication of the end of a harmony. Although not all aspects of the notation are completely understood today, players who become familiar with the preludes find them to be remarkable examples of a tradition that embodied both improvisation and notation.

Declamation and recitative

With monody and the new expressive singing advocated by Caccini came a type of declamatory delivery called recitative. Although notated in the same manner as other music, its performance was governed by conventions that allowed the singer freedom to depart from the notated rhythms in order to follow the natural accents of the text, and to determine the speed of declamation according to the meaning and desired expression. Monteverdi called this style of singing *stile rappresentativo* (literally, theatrical or declamatory style) of which the *lettera amorosa*, "Se i languidi miei sguardi," from his seventh book of madrigals (1619),[5] is a well-known example. Also written in *stile rappresentativo* is the "Lamento della Ninfa" (*Madrigali guerrieri et [sic] amorosi, libro ottavo*, Venice, 1638),[6] a passionate lament by the lovelorn shepherdess set over a passacaglia (descending tetrachord) bass. The introduction and epilogue, sung by three men, should be performed metrically [*tempo de la mano*], according to Monteverdi's indication in the partbooks. The nymph's lament with interjections from three other singers, who follow the costumed nymph as she wanders mournfully, should be sung freely "in the tempo of the soul [*a tempo del'affetto del animo*]."

In the early seventeenth century, recitative and aria are not always necessarily clearly distinguished. Arias tend to have a more obvious melodic contour, both in the voice and accompaniment, and many are in triple meter. Recitative usually has a more static bass, is notated in 4/4 or duple meter, and its text is often more laden with emotion. Either may use a repeating pattern of strophic variations, in which the bass line is repeated several times, often using long notes, while the vocal line varies above it. An example of a piece incorporating features of both aria and recitative is Orfeo's lament, "Possente spirto" (Appendix A). Its bass is predominantly strophic like an aria, but the heartfelt pleas to Charon and the declamatory nature of the ornate melodic line are close to the *stile recitativo*.

After the middle of the seventeenth century, recitative and aria are more clearly distinguished in opera, oratorio, and cantatas, and the specific conventions for performing recitative can be more easily differentiated. In opera, most of the action was embodied in the recitative, along with the dialogue and advancement of the plot. The arias, on the other hand, provided contrast by suspending the plot momentarily so that the characters could give release to their passions, feelings, and desires. The distinction is similar in cantatas and oratorios, but the recitative is usually less action-ridden and predominantly narrative in these genres. Recitative was delivered in a relatively rapid, declamatory manner according to the natural accents of the text, but we shall see that different conventions governed its performance according to genre and country.

PERFORMING RECITATIVE IN THE ITALIAN STYLE

Italian composers notated their recitative in common time, with a bass line in relatively long note values. The notation, however, bore little resemblance to actual performance. Vocal treatises by Tosi, Mancini, and others describe the manner of performance which became conventional after 1700. Singers were expected to add appoggiaturas in certain situations, such as when there was a leap of a third followed by two repeated notes, or on a long note, and at the final cadence, which was written either with a falling third or fourth in the vocal line and performed with an appoggiatura in either case. The appoggiatura was not to be performed in a perfunctory manner, but with proper stress, volume, and length, and according to Mancini, the recitative was to be done with a variety of nuance in tone and rhythm so that it does not sound continuously sung.

The vocal part usually was restricted to the compass of a fourth and contained many repeated notes, which contributed to a fairly rapid delivery. Composers chose the tessitura according to the most comfortable register for each voice, which was called the *voce di petto*, or chest voice. The other registers, the *voce di testa*, a light head voice suited to ornamentation, and the *falsetto*, formed in the throat, were usually avoided except for unusual circumstances such as a sudden cry or outburst. Although the three registers were identified and described separately, eighteenth-century writers such as Quantz and Burney stress the importance of being able to unite the three registers with a "carrying of the voice" called portamento.[7] The modern meaning of the word portamento as a sliding or gliding connection between two notes did not become established until well into the nineteenth century.

The accompaniment of recitative was most often entrusted to harpsichord and cello, except in sacred music where the organ replaced the harpsichord. Several treatises describe the conventions of recitative accompaniment in detail. An early example is Francesco Gasparini's *L'armonico pratico al cembalo* (1708). He cautions that the singer should be free "to take the lead, singing at his discretion and in accord with the expression of the words." Chords in the accompaniment are to be arpeggiated, particularly when they are consonant, but he warns against too much arpeggiation, and against ascending and descending scale passages, since these only display "facility" and "create confusion."

Descriptive sources for the accompaniment of Italian recitative toward the middle of the eighteenth century show that the general principles of accompaniment remain unchanged. Quantz provides directions for accompanying a passage of recitative (Example 7-1). He advises that the accompanist should guide the singer by anticipating notes and playing them before the singer enters. The accompanist thereby "puts them into his mouth for him by striking the

Example 7-1. How to accompany a recitative, from Quantz's *On Playing the Flute* (1752).

chord with a quick arpeggiation in such fashion that, where possible, the singer's first note lies in the upper part; immediately afterwards he should strike separately several of the following intervals that appear in the vocal part (Quantz, 265)." Quantz notates the accompaniment in full, in order to illustrate the technique. From his accompaniment, we note that three- and four-note chords may be played with each hand, and that the bass may be doubled at the octave occasionally, filling in the space with notes of the chord. As in Geminiani's example discussed earlier (see chapter 5, Example 5-1), the added notes in the left hand (notated in black) are probably meant to be released quickly. The chord in measure 2 suggests that ties in the bass should not prevent the player from restriking the harmony if the occasion warrants. Quantz's advice for a quick arpeggiation of each chord produces a full sonority from the harpsichord and a volume sufficient to be heard easily by the singer even when separated from the instrument.

Convention also governed the performance of cadences in Italian recitative, which were performed either after the singer finished a phrase or simultaneously with the singer's last notes. In opera, the cadence was frequently aligned with the final two notes of the singer's phrase whether or not it was notated in that manner. Cadences foreshortened in this way provided a forward drive that was particularly suited to the stage, but in other circumstances such as the cantata or oratorio, foreshortened cadences were not necessarily obligatory. Telemann provides examples of such cadences in his *Singe-, Spiel-, und Generalbass-Übungen* (Hamburg, 1733–1734), which he says would be used in opera but not in cantatas (Example 7-2).

Example 7-2. Telemann's foreshortened cadence in recitative, from *Singe-, Spiel-, und Generalbass-Übungen* (Hamburg, 1733–34), no. 40.

PERFORMING RECITATIVE IN THE FRENCH STYLE

In France, a different tradition of recitative performance became established in Lully's works, and it remained current until at least the middle of the eighteenth century. French composers followed the accentuation of the text in their notation, employing different meters whenever required. The most common meters are ₵, 2, and 3/4 (or 3). The declamatory nature of recitative still necessitated a certain freedom from the notated rhythms, but French composers usually attempted to follow the accentuations of speech in their notation. In most cases, a half note in ₵ or 2 was approximately equivalent to a quarter note in 3/4. Differentiating French recitative from its Italian counterpart are the more active bass line, wider range in the vocal part, and more frequent ornamentation. Although French recitative was also declaimed [*débité*], critics of the first half of the eighteenth century observed that Italian recitative was performed at a faster pace than French recitative. Between Lully and Rameau, French recitative shows a trend toward a reduction of note values, but since the pace was slower, the apparent result in performance was a slowing down of the declamation. According to Rousseau's *Lettre sur la musique française* (1753), trills and appoggiaturas were performed in a "more languishing" manner in his day than in Lully's, when recitative was "quicker and less dragging; one sang it less and declaimed it more (Rousseau, 61f)."

The type of ornamentation applied to French recitative is shown in a passage from Lully's *Atys* (Example 7-3), included in Bérard's *L'art du chant* (1755). (See also chapter 8 and Example 8-4 for further explanation of Bérard's ornamentation.) A quick, short trill (marked +) that adds stress without interfering with the declamation was the preferred type for recitative, according to Montéclair (*Principes de musique*, 1736). The *accent* on a long note, which is a rising inflection or "caressing" of the upper note, was added by Bérard on accented notes that carry an expressive meaning (marked T, as on *troublez*, m. 3). Because of the greater range of French recitative, singers used different registers of the voice, although singers were cautioned against mixing the natural voice with falsetto in recitative.

The accompaniment in French opera was performed by members of the *petit choeur*, a small number of instrumentalists close to the harpsichord who were responsible for the more delicate accompaniments in recitatives and some airs. Recitative was most often accompanied by some of the basso continuo instruments (including theorbo, viola da gamba or cello, and harpsichord). The theorbo (or two theorbos until about 1723) played either in addition to the harpsichord or substituted for it in certain places. Pierre Bonnet (*Histoire de musique et de ses effets*, 1715) observed that the combination of viol, harpsichord, and theorbo sometimes caused confusion.[8] Although the use of theorbos in opera declined in France after 1720, they were probably retained longer in England and Italy, for they can be seen in paintings and engravings of opera performances. The painting in Figure 4 by Marco Ricci (1676–1730) is one of several entitled "Rehearsal of an Opera," painted during and after his visits to London from 1708 to 1710 or 1711 and from 1712 to 1716. This example, probably executed in Italy after his return,[9] includes a theorbo in the ensemble of continuo players and singers.

For violent sounds

It is necessary to force air out of the lungs very quickly, to pronounce in a hard and obscure manner, and to double the consonants rather strongly.

Translation: Heavens! What vapor surrounds me! All my senses are disturbed. I tremble, I shiver, I shake, and all at once a diabolical fervor comes to ignite my blood and devour my heart. Gods! What do I see? Heaven arms itself against the earth. What chaos! What noise!

Example 7-3. Lully, "Ciel, quelle vapeur m'environne," recitative from *Atys*, with ornaments from Bérard's *L'art du chant* (Paris, 1755).

Figure 4. Marco Ricci (1676–1730), "Rehearsal of an Opera."

Other rhythmic alterations

The three main types of rhythmic alteration that affect the expression and character of a piece are (1) *notes inégales*, (2) overdotting (sometimes also called double dotting), and finally (3) alignment of certain rhythmic figures with triplets. In many cases, the performer must weigh the possible interpretations and choose the one that best suits the character of the music.

NOTES INÉGALES

The practice of performing pairs of notes unequally, usually by lengthening the first and shortening the second, was widespread throughout the baroque era. Taken in its broadest sense, this application of inequality often allowed (but did not require) notes to be dotted when they were not notated as such, as in Caccini's or Frescobaldi's music, according to the expression the soloist wished to add. In early seventeenth-century Italian music, this sort of rhythmic alteration was permitted in either the long–short or short–long variety, and it was performed in a sharply dotted or accented manner. Such dotted rhythms also suit the natural accents of the English language, and Purcell used them liberally in declamatory pieces, where they are specifically written and not added at the performer's discretion.

Notes inégales differed from the Italian type of dotted rhythm described above in being a practice associated primarily with French music, or with music whose character or performance was intended to be in the French style. Because the inequality was an integral part of the expressive character of the music, it was considered obligatory in many circumstances, yet the actual degree of inequality was left to the performer.

The practice of *notes inégales* was described by many theorists of the seventeenth and eighteenth centuries, and there is evidence that it was known and practiced outside of France, at least when music in the French style was performed. It may be defined as the unequal interpretation of rhythms that are notated equally. Normally, inequality falls upon the smaller note values within a piece, and is applied to conjunct notes, making them fall gracefully and gently into pairs of notes. Most suited to moderate tempos, inequality may also be used at slower and faster speeds, but it is less appropriate when tempos are either very fast or very slow.

Thus, the tempo and character of the music must be the first concern when one considers the degree of inequality. It is most suited to pieces whose melody is graceful, elegant, or flowing, and whose character is gentle and pleasing. As St. Lambert (1702) writes, *notes inégales* were used on certain notes "because the inequality gives them more grace." Although certain rules may serve as a guide to the specific application of inequality, performers who keep in mind the general characteristics associated with *inégalité* will quickly learn to use it in appropriate contexts. In other types of pieces, such as a march or a spritely *giga* with disjunct motion, for example, inequality does not apply, since the character of the piece lies outside the graceful, flowing character associated with inequality.

Inequality is performed by prolonging the first of two notes (or, more rarely, the reverse), and also by giving it stress. The degree of inequality may vary from barely audible to quite pronounced. It generally applies to one rhythmic level within a piece or movement, and most often the smallest note values receive the inequality. In most cases, this will be eighth or sixteenth notes, but in some meters (such as 3/2) quarter notes may be played unequally. The more subtle the inequality, the more likely it is to be accomplished by gentle stress rather than obvious rhythmic prolongation. It is done in this case with the tonguing or bow stroke, and the rhythm is scarcely affected.

In vocal music, inequality is well-suited to the French language and enhances its fluid pronunciation. It is also appropriate in sacred French music (with a Latin text), although motets of the eighteenth century are often conspicuously Italianate in character and thus would not require it. Other features that would limit or exclude the use of inequality are: (1) any indication to the contrary added by the composer, such as the direction *"notes égales"* or *"marqué,"* or the use of dots above notes that would otherwise be played unequally, (2) notes that do not fall easily into groups of two, as for example, in leaping passages, or many repeated notes or triplets, and (3) a quick tempo.

Occasionally one finds that inequality may be implied when dotted notes are written. One must be cautious about interpreting inequality in this case; the best guide is the character of the music, which must be gentle or flowing for inequality to be appropriate. A *musette en rondeau* for harpsichord by Rameau (*Pièces de clavecin*, Paris, 1724), includes passages in eighth notes, but when he used the piece again in his *opéra-ballet*, *Les fêtes d'Hébé* (1739), he adopted a dotted notation (Example 7-4). Although it is possible that two different rhythmic interpretations are meant, this seems unlikely. Rather, the two notations are merely different ways of writing the inequality that would be expected in performance. Another opportunity for comparing the use of inequality by singers and instrumentalists is the menuet for harpsichord, which is also both an instrumental and vocal piece in the prologue to *Castor et Pollux* (1737) (Appendix A).

Although Corrette's treatise for the flute (*Méthode raisonnée pour apprendre à jouer de la flute traversière*) was published in Paris in 1773, the examples he

Example 7-4 a, b. Rameau, *musette en rondeau* in two versions: (a) as a harpsichord piece (*Pièces de clavecin*, 1724), and (b) as an orchestral piece in *Les fêtes d'Hébé* (Paris, 1739).

includes are chosen from works of some thirty years before that date, and his advice is thus useful for interpreting French music of the mid-eighteenth century. He discusses inequality as a way of dotting notes [*pointer*] which is done in certain meters. In the meter 2, for example, which is used for "*rigaudons, gavottes, bourées* and *cotillons,*" he notes that "it is necessary to dot the eighth notes two by two, that is to say, make the first long and the second short." In Italian music, he considers inequality possible but optional. "The meters 2/4 and 2/8 are found in Italian Allegros and Prestos from sonatas and concertos. It is necessary to play eighth notes equally, and to dot the sixteenth notes; one sometimes also plays them equally in sonatas."

OVERDOTTING

Dotted notes in baroque music were lengthened in certain circumstances, and the note following the dot was shortened by half its value or more, depending upon the tempo. Although the variable length of the dotted note can be viewed as a type of pronounced inequality, it is more easily understood as having an entirely different effect. Overdotting was applied to pieces whose character was noble, stately, slow, marchlike, or vigorous and sharply articulated. Pieces in which overdotting applies are thus fundamentally different in character from the gentle, flowing, elegant pieces that require inequality.

RHYTHMIC ALIGNMENT WITH TRIPLETS

Several different rhythmic notations may be used in pieces which have triplet subdivisions, and these notations may cause modern performers some concern unless they are interpreted with some latitude. In most cases, when triplet rhythms are predominant, other rhythmic figures, such as eighth notes or those that consist of a dotted eighth and sixteenth note, will be aligned with the triplets. In the *giga* (last movement) of Corelli's Sonata Op. 5, No. 5 (Appendix A), the quarter notes in the continuo should be played as if they were dotted (in 12/8) and the eighth notes in mm. 10–12 aligned with the third note of the violin's triplets. In the last movement of Bach's Brandenburg Concerto No. 5 (BWV 1050),[10] the sixteenth note in the dotted-eighth-and-sixteenth-note figures would be played with the third triplet, in order to preserve the character which, like Corelli's finale, is a flowing, Italianate *giga*.

The same principle of aligning sixteenth notes with triplets would apply in the first movement (*larghetto*) of Handel's Sonata for recorder in A minor (Op. 1, No. 4), where the resulting spirit is gentle, with the triplets giving the movement a rather easygoing manner (Example 7-5). The most important consideration is that a single character or affect be expressed by resolving any conflicts in the notation. Baroque composers usually regarded the use of mixed rhythmic notations as a convenience and assumed that performers would understand the desired expression and align rhythms accordingly.

Example 7-5. Handel, Larghetto (first movement) from Sonata in A minor (Op. 1, No. 4) for recorder and continuo, with triplets and dotted notes (to be aligned with the triplets).

Summary and final thoughts

There are many examples of inexact notations of rhythms in the baroque era that might cause the modern performer some confusion unless certain conventions of the time are known. Two types of rhythmic alteration were used especially in French music: overdotting (a sharply dotted style for ouvertures and other noble, stately, or grand pieces), and inequality (the gentle grouping of notes, usually by lengthening the first of a pair).

Unmeasured preludes, notated predominantly in whole notes, are an unusual example of the extreme freedom sometimes accorded the solo performer. Other examples of passages that are meant to sound improvisatory, though written in normal rhythmic values, can be found in instrumental sonatas, where they are sometimes marked *recitativo* or adagio. In most cases, the accompaniment either rests or plays a pedal note or other slow-moving harmony, leaving the soloist free to depart from the notated rhythms in a manner that sounds improvisatory (for example, mm. 30–46 in Buxtehude's Sonata in A, Appendix A).

Bibliographical notes

A valuable guide to rhythmic alteration in French music is Betty Bang Mather's *Interpretation of French Music*, which includes a bibliography of seventeenth- and eighteenth-century treatises and modern sources. Davitt Moroney offers the results of his research and experience with playing unmeasured preludes in an excellent preface to the revised edition of Louis Couperin's music. The preludes in Alan Curtis's edition are based on a single manuscript source (the Parville manuscript in the Music Library of the University of California, Berkeley) and offer a fascinating comparison with those in Moroney's edition.

The interpretation of rhythm in the French ouverture and the French practice of *notes inégales* are the subjects of considerable discussion and controversy in the literature. Frederick Neumann questions the theoretical evidence about inequality, and in a recent essay, "The *Notes Inégales* revisited," he contends that *notes inégales* should not be used in music by non-French composers even when they wrote in a French style. Robert Donington offers considerable theoretical evidence supporting the use of inequality in both Italian and German music in "A Footnote to Inequality," which is Appendix 8 (pp. 665–670) in the new revised edition of his *Interpretation of Early Music* (see Donington, Appendix B, below). Michael Collins and David Fuller also counter Neumann with support from numerous treatises and musical evidence.

An excellent discussion of notational practices concerning the dot is Fuller's "The 'Dotted Style' in Bach, Handel, and Scarlatti." Neumann argues (not entirely convincingly) for an interpretation based upon strict adherence to notation in Bach's *Ouverture nach französischer Art* (BWV 831) for harpsichord.

FOR FURTHER STUDY

Best, Terence. "Interpreting Handel's Rhythmic Notation—Some Reflections on Modern Practice." In *Handel Tercentenary Collection*. Ed. Stanley Sadie and Anthony Hicks, 279–290. Macmillan: Basingstoke, Hampshire, 1987.

Byrt, John. "*Notes Inégales*—Some Misconceptions?" *JAMS* 20 no. 3 (1967): 476–480.

Collins, Michael. "In Defense of the French Trill." *JAMS* 26 no. 3 (1973): 405–439.

_____ . "Notes Inégales: a Re-Examination." *JAMS* 20 no. 3 (1967): 481–485.

_____ . "The Performance of Triplets in the Seventeenth and Eighteenth Centuries." *JAMS* 19 no. 3 (1966): 281–328.

_____ . "A Reconsideration of French Overdotting." *ML* 50 no. 1 (1969): 111–123.

Couperin, Louis. *Pièces de clavecin*. Ed. Paul Brunold, revised by Davitt Moroney. Monaco: Edition de l'Oiseau Lyre, 1985.

_____ . *Pièces de clavecin*. Ed. Alan Curtis. Paris: Heugel, 1970.

Dean, Winton. "The Performance of Recitative in Late Baroque Opera." *ML* 58 no. 4 (1977): 389–402.

Donington, Robert. "A Problem of Inequality." *MQ* 53 (1967): 503–517.

Fuller, David. "Dotting, the 'French Style' and Frederick Neumann's Counter-Reformation." *EM* 5 (1977): 517–543.

_____ . "Notes and *Inégales* Unjoined: Defending a Definition." *JM* 7 (Winter, 1989): 21–28.

_____ . "The 'Dotted Style' in Bach, Handel, and Scarlatti." In *Bach, Handel, Scarlatti: Tercenenary Essays*. Ed. Peter Williams, 99–117. Cambridge: Cambridge University Press, 1985.

Gustafson, Bruce. "A Letter from Mr Lebègue Concerning his Preludes." *Recherches* 17 (1977): 7–14.

Hansell, Sven. "The acciaccatura in recitatives: a question of what works?" *Pergolesi Studies* 2[1989]: 110–115.

Mather, Betty Bang. *Interpretation of French Music from 1675 to 1775 for Woodwind and Other Performers*. New York: McGinnis & Marx, 1973.

Mather, Betty Bang, and David Lasocki. *The Art of Preluding, 1700–1830, for Flutists, Oboists, Clarinettists, and Other Performers*. New York: McGinnis & Marx, 1984.

Moroney, Davitt. "The Performance of Unmeasured Harpsichord Preludes." *EM* 4 (April 1976): 143–151.

Neumann, Frederick. *Essays in Performance Practice*. Ann Arbor: UMI Research Press, 1982.

———. "Facts and Fiction about Overdotting." *MQ* 63 no. 2 (1977): 155–185.

———. "Misconceptions about the French Trill in the Seventeenth and Eighteenth Centuries." *MQ* 50 no. 2 (1964): 188–206 (reprinted in *Essays*).

———. *New Essays on Performance Practice*. Ann Arbor, UMI Research Press, 1989.

———. "Once More: the 'French Ouverture Style'." *EM* 7 (1979): 39–45 (reprinted in *Essays*).

———. "The Dotted Note and the So-Called French Style." Transl. Raymond Harris and Edmund Shay. *EM* 5 (July 1977): 310–324 (reprinted in *Essays*; from an article originally in French in *RdeM* 51 no. 1 [1965]: 66–87).

———. "The *Notes Inégales* Revisited." *Journal of Musicology* 6 (1988): 137–149.

———. "The Question of Rhythm in the Two Versions of Bach's French Overture, BWV 831." In *Studies in Renaissance and Baroque Music in Honor of Arthur Mendel*. Ed. Robert L. Marshall, 183–194. Kassel: Bärenreiter, 1974.

Pfeiffer, Christel. "Das französische Prelude non mesuré für Cembalo: Notation, Interpretation, Einfluss auf Froberger, Bach, Handel." *Neue Zeitschrift für Musikwissenschaft* 62 no. 2 (1979): 132–136.

Pont, Graham. "Rhythmic Alteration and the Majestic." *Studies in Music* 12 (1978): 68–100.

———. "French Ouvertures at the Keyboard: 'How Handel Rendered the Playing of Them'." *Musicology* 6 (1980): 29–50.

Rosow, Lois. "French Baroque Recitative as an Expression of Tragic Declamation." *EM* 11 (1983): 468–479.

Seares, Margaret. "Aspects of Performance Practice in the Recitatives of Jean-Baptiste Lully." *Studies in Music* 8 (1974): 8–16.

Weber, Edith, ed. *L'interprétation de la musique française aux XVIIème et XVIIIème siècles*. Colloques internationaux du Centre National de la Recherche Scientifique, Paris, Oct. 20–26, 1969. Paris: Centre Nationale de Recherche Scientifique, 1974.

Wolf, Robert Peter. "Metrical Relationships in French Recitative of the Seventeenth and Eighteenth Centuries." *Recherches* 18 (1978): 29–49.

NOTES TO CHAPTER 7

1. J.-P. Rameau, *Pièces de clavecin*, ed. Kenneth Gilbert (Paris: Heugel, n.d., 2.)
2. Claude-Bénigne Balbastre, *Pièces de clavecin, d'orgue, et de forte piano*, ed. Alan Curtis (Paris: Heugel, 1974), 50.
3. DeMachy, *Pièces de violle* (Paris, 1685; R Geneva: Minkoff, 1973), 4.
4. See the article by Bruce Gustafson in the bibliography at the end of this chapter.
5. *Concerto. Settimo libro de Madrigali* (Venice, 1619), *MonteverdiW*, v. 7, p. 160.
6. *MonteverdiW*, v. 8, part 2, p. 286.
7. Burney, *The Present State of Music*, 19; *Quantz*, 300.
8. Bonnet-Bourdelot, 1:297f; also in *MacClintock*, 243f.
9. For reproductions of Ricci's other paintings on the same subject, see Richard Leppert, "Imagery, Musical Confrontation and Cultural Difference in Early Eighteenth-Century London," *EM* 14 (1986), 323–345; and Eric Walter White, "The Rehearsal of an Opera," *Theatre Notebook* 14 (1960), 79–90. Two of Ricci's paintings are also reproduced in Tilden A. Russell, "The Development of the Cello Endpin," *Imago musicae* 4 (1987), 335–356.
10. *BachW*, series 7, v. 2, ed. Heinrich Besseler (Kassel: Bärenreiter, 1956), 176.

8

Ornamentation

In today's music, the roles of performer and composer are usually separate: composers write what they expect performers to play, and performers do not depart significantly from the written text. In baroque music, however, the performer and composer shared a more equal role in the compositional process, and two performances of the same piece could therefore be vastly different.

There were a number of different ways in which the composer and performer shared the stage. In solo works, the composer and performer were often the same individual. In concertos and operas, the composer often led performances from the harpsichord. A score used by the composer may be lacking in many details that one would consider crucial for modern performances. In Handel's organ concertos, for example, passages that were improvised by the composer are omitted in the manuscripts. If the score or parts were published, more information may have been included, since performances outside the composer's own circle were expected. Often such information is provided in an introduction or foreword. If a work survives only in manuscript copies, the composer's intentions may be much more difficult to trace.

In addition to such intentional omissions in manuscripts, some notational obscurities result from the stylistic conventions of the time. In the slow movement of Italian sonatas, for example, composers often intentionally wrote only a bass and a simple melodic line, and they expected the performer to embellish the melody. Not only did the performer and composer both participate in the creative process, but the performer and instrument were also united in the aim of expressing the passion or affect within the music.

In some types of music, such as most French solo music, ornamentation was usually indicated by the composer with a variety of different signs, but elsewhere, such as in Italian arias or sonatas, proper ornamentation depended upon the knowledge and invention of the performer and was rarely indicated. Depending upon how elaborate the ornamentation might be, a performer might plan it in advance, but it must sound as fresh as if it were improvised on the spot. The most elaborate ornamentations belong to two types of baroque pieces: the slow movement of an Italian sonata, and the return (da capo) of the A section in an aria. Enough eyewitness accounts and written-out ornamentations survive to give us some idea about how such pieces were ornamented.[1]

The early baroque period

In madrigals and other music of the late sixteenth century, florid ornamentation was frequently added by the performers. Consisting largely of running or passing notes, these ornaments or diminutions were often elaborate, especially when added in several parts at once. From manuals on diminution practice by dalla Casa (1584), Bassano (1585), and others, we know that ornamentation was practiced in both vocal and instrumental music by ensembles as well as soloists.

The new seventeenth-century concept of the solo voice as the ideal vehicle for expression, advocated by Caccini and the members of the Florentine camerata, gave a new role to ornamentation. In Caccini's new style, ornamentation of the running, virtuosic type called diminution was replaced by ornamentation of a dynamic or rhythmic origin, often placed on single notes, or affecting only a few notes. Like the sixteenth-century diminutions, the *trillo*, *gruppo*, and other ornaments were usually not written in the music, but their placement was governed by the meaning and expression of the text, and also to an extent by the technical suitability of singing ornaments on some vowels.

Caccini described the elements of the new style of singing in the foreword to his *Le nuove musiche* (1602). He characterizes diminution as more proper for wind and string instruments than for the voice, although he admits the use of some divisions or diminutions in less passionate music, where they may be sung on long syllables and at the final cadences. Speaking of the solo voice as the ideal vehicle for passionate expression, he advocates "talking in harmony" with "a certain noble neglect of the song," reminiscent of the style of singing recitative. Certain ornaments such as the *messa di voce*, *esclamatione*, *trillo*, and *gruppo* are most appropriate to passionate texts. The *messa di voce* consisted of a crescendo and diminuendo on a long note, and the *esclamatione* was a type of accent followed by a diminuendo of the voice (see also chapter 2, "Written and unwritten dynamic nuances in the seventeenth century"). A third type of attack on a note was called "tuning the voice," which consisted either of beginning lightly from a third below and moving quickly up to the note, or beginning the note and adding a crescendo. He provides an illustration in staff notation of how the *trillo* and *gruppo* should be sung (Example 8-1a), and how the rhythm may be altered for more expressive delivery (Example 8-1b). He also includes three of his own compositions ("Cor mio," "Ahi, dispietato Amor," and "Deh, dove son

Example 8-1a, b. (a) The performance of the *trillo* and the *gruppo*, and (b) rhythmic alteration according to Caccini's *Le nuove musiche* (1602).

fuggiti,") with written-out ornamentation and indications for adding the *esclama-tione* and other nuances. In his songs, the *trillo* is used on an accented syllable within a phrase or on the penultimate note of a phrase. In "Deh, dove son fuggiti" (Example 8-2), the *esclamatione* is used several times at the beginning of a phrase on a long note, and less frequently on a long note within a phrase. Caccini recommends the use of a theorbo to accompany the voice. He adds that bass notes or notes of the chord may be restruck as necessary, but sometimes he places ties in the bass to indicate that only notes above the bass should enter after the bass is struck.

Translation: O where have the eyes whose rays I turned into ashes fled?

Example 8-2. Caccini, "Deh, dove son fuggiti," with indications for expressive delivery, from *Le nuove musiche* (1602).

Claudio Monteverdi also incorporated the new expressive vocal style in certain madrigals and motets, and in his operas. A few ornaments of the type Caccini describes are written in the vocal parts, and their placement can furnish a guide to how they may be added in other passages. That the expressive, nuanced style of delivery has a place in sacred music as well can be seen in some of Monteverdi's solo motets, such as "Laudate Dominum" for solo voice (soprano or tenor) and basso continuo, in which a *trillo* is written out on the word "cimbalis" and some florid *passaggi* are used on "alleluia" (Example 8-3 a, b). In pieces that belong to the theatrical style, or *genere rappresentativo*, such as *Il Ballo*

Example 8-3 a, b. Monteverdi, "Laudate Dominum" for solo voice (soprano or tenor) and continuo, with ornaments written out by the composer.

dell'Ingrate (*Madrigali guerrieri et (sic) amorosi*, 1638),[2] ornamentation of the type described by Caccini is particularly appropriate to enhance the expression of the text.

An unusual example of a written-out ornamentation provided by Monteverdi is Orfeo's well-known song, "Possente spirto,"[3] beseeching Caronte to grant him passage into the underworld to retrieve his lost Euridice. In the printed score of *Orfeo* (1609), Monteverdi provided two vocal lines and indicated that Orfeo is to sing one of them "to the sound of an organ with wooden pipes and a chitarrone" (as continuo instruments). The ornaments are fully written out in one of the two parts, and the other is left plain, presumably so that a singer could improvise his own ornaments. The song consists of five strophes, four of which are punctuated by instrumental ritornellos (Appendix A). Orfeo sings his moving lament in recitative style over a bass that repeats with slight rhythmic changes for each strophe. Of the three eleven-syllable (*endecasillabo*) lines, the third is the most elaborately ornamented in each strophe. In the first two strophes, some of the written-out ornaments are passing notes (m. 8, on *al*tra), a short *ribattuta* (m. 12, presume), or a *trillo* (m. 8, al*tra*). The third strophe (mm. 29–47), addressed to Euridice, is more elaborately ornamented, with dotted rhythms, repeated notes, and *passaggi*. Ornaments are written out in the instrumental ritornellos as well, especially cadential trills, and also some other figures similar to those in the vocal part. Some passages are also left plain, especially in the last strophe (mm. 68–80), and it may be assumed that the singer would add graces of a dynamic nature here (on a stressed note, for example), such as the *messa di voce*.

The expressive style of singing advocated by Caccini spread to Germany with composers such as Heinrich Schütz, who studied with Monteverdi, and also to England, where Purcell adapted some of the characteristics of Caccini's rhythms and ornamentation for use with English texts. The style of solo singing current in the first decade of the seventeenth century was transferred to solo violin, cornetto, and other instruments soon after, and the same type of ornamentation became the expressive ideal for these instruments as well. In Italian instrumental music of the early seventeenth century written in the new style by Dario Castello, Giovanni Paolo Cima, and others, a few ornaments may be indicated by signs, such as *t* or *tr*, but in general, performers may use Caccini's instructions as a guide for adding the *trillo*, *gruppo*, and *ribattuta* on long or otherwise expressive notes, and on the penultimate note at a cadence.

Italian ornamentation after 1660

The most common signs encountered in seventeenth-century music are those for a type of trill (usually *t*, +, or *tr*). In the early seventeenth century the sign may be taken to be the *trillo* or single-note repetition described by Caccini. In music from the second half of the century, the sign more likely indicates a trill between two notes, frequently starting on the written pitch (or main note) and alternating with the note a half step or whole step above. The trill may be varied as to length, stress, or speed, according to the word on which it is placed and the rhythmic and harmonic context.

Composers sometimes wrote out ornamented passages fully, and once these are recognized as such, performers may be allowed some liberty in interpreting the rhythmic notation in order to make it sound improvised. Examples of such passages, frequently accompanied by a static bass line, can be found in the sonatas of Biagio Marini, Heinrich Biber, and Dieterich Buxtehude, where they may be transitional sections between two movements of a more contrapuntal or dancelike character.

In Italian music, ornamentation is rarely written out except for a few trills that may be indicated with signs, or appoggiaturas that may be written out or indicated with a small note slurred to the main one. There are many musical circumstances that allow free ornamentation to be added, as for example in arias, particularly those with a repeated refrain or a da capo. The slow movements of instrumental works, too, call for the addition of some ornamentation. Performers were often expected to invent free ornamentation of an elaborate type that required a knowledge of harmony, since its main features were runs, arpeggios, leaps, and rapid figuration.

Numerous written-out ornamentations for Corelli's violin sonatas are preserved, furnishing an excellent model to modern players who wish to learn the style of elaborate ornamentation practiced by seventeenth-century Italian violinists.[4] The earliest of these is the fourth edition (1710) of Corelli's sonatas of Op. 5 published by Roger in Amsterdam, with ornaments for some slow movements supposedly by the composer. They furnish a wealth of examples showing the variety and extent of elaboration of the original melodic line, which is shown on a separate staff (see his Sonata No. 5, Appendix A). The more elaborate, running ornaments may consist of eight to twenty-four notes within the time of a quarter note, and a repeated melodic idea or a sequence is usually ornamented differently each time. Long notes are rarely ornamented, perhaps because a *messa di voce* or other dynamic nuance would be considered appropriate, and cadences are usually left plain except for the addition of a trill or appoggiatura. The adagios in 3/4 are more simply ornamented than those in Common time, usually with sixteenth notes as the most elaborate addition. This feature suggests that the tempo may have been somewhat faster in the triple-meter slow movements than those in Common time.

Telemann's collection of *Zwölf Methodische Sonaten* provides examples of how a slow movement may be ornamented in the Italian manner. The first set of six sonatas "for violin or flute and basso continuo" was published in 1728, and the second set of six "for flute or violin and basso continuo" followed four years later.[5] They are pedagogical in nature, as the title indicates, and in the first slow movement of each sonata the plain melodic line and an ornamentation are included on separate staves. Players can add appropriate ornamentation of their own invention to the other movements. All but four of the ornamented slow movements are in Common time, and most are either adagios (sonatas 1, 2, and 8) or andantes (nos. 4, 9, 11, and 12). The others include one grave in 3/4 (no. 3), two largos in 6/8 (no. 5) and 3/2 (no. 10), a cantabile in Common time (no. 6), and a siciliana in 12/8 (no. 7). Thus they provide examples of the diversity one finds in slow movements from Italian sonatas of the period.

Ornamented slow movements by Telemann, in comparison to those of Corelli, usually contain a more consistent amount of ornamentation in each phrase. Like Corelli's, the cadences and points of rest within phrases are not elaborately decorated, though they may have an appoggiatura or a trill. Whether or not the plain melodic line includes triplets, Telemann frequently introduces them. Their presence in pieces with eighth-note and sixteenth-note motion is characteristic of Telemann's music and frequently associated with the *galant* style, though triplets are not usually as prominent in the works of Italian composers and were entirely absent in Corelli's ornamentations. Another departure from

Corelli's practice is that Telemann's elaborations may be placed on the last note of a phrase. In the first movement from the Sonata No. 2 in A major (Example 8-4), some eighth notes are ornamented as broken chords in thirty-second notes (mm. 1–2), and triplets are added for passing motion (mm. 1, 7, 9) and as moving melodic notes (mm. 5–6). The result in Telemann's sonatas is often a pleasing consistency of ornamentation requiring melodic invention on the part of the player, with somewhat less of the improvisatory effect that Corelli's ornamentations offer the listener.

Much of the documentation concerning ornaments used in singing during the first quarter of the eighteenth century is preserved in Pier Francesco Tosi's important treatise, *Opinioni de'cantori antichi, e moderni* (1723; translated by Galliard as *Observations on the Florid Song*, 1743). Although Tosi's observations must be regarded as reflections of his own somewhat conservative taste, they nevertheless furnish useful guidelines for singers concerning style, delivery, and ornamentation.

Among the most important ornaments Tosi describes is the appoggiatura, "a note added by the Singer, for the arriving more gracefully to the following Note, either in rising or falling (p. 31)." One "leans" on the appoggiatura, dwelling longer on the ornament than the note itself, according to Tosi, and the same may be done at the beginning of a trill or a mordent.

Concerning the da capo aria, Tosi recommended the addition of a few discreet ornaments in the A section, and more in the B section and the da capo. He writes:

> In the first [section] they require nothing but the simplest Orna-
> ments, of a Good Taste and few, that the Composition may remain
> simple, plain, and pure; in the second they expect, that to this Purity
> some artful Graces be added, by which the Judicious may hear, that
> the Ability of the Singers is greater; and, in repeating the *Air*, he that
> does not vary it for the better, is no great Master (Tosi, 93f).

In the da capo aria, it was customary for singers to add one or more cadenzas at the end of each section (and sometimes also within the sections), but Tosi felt that singers of the time abused the custom by making them too long and adding too many. He preferred that a cadenza of no longer than a single breath be added only at the final cadence in the da capo section. The aria, "Sirti, scogli, tempeste," from Handel's *Flavio* (Appendix A) has a pause for a cadenza near the end of the A section (m. 32); the approach to the cadence at the end of the B section would also allow the possibility of elaboration (m. 47, beat 4 and m. 48, beat 3), making it possible to sing a total of four cadenzas (including the one in the da capo). The best place to add one, however, would be at the end of the A section da capo. Surviving cadenzas sung by the soprano Faustina Bordoni and the castrato Carlo Broschi (called Farinelli) illustrate that singers frequently went well beyond Tosi's (and Handel's) modest guidelines. An aria sung by Farinelli in Geminiano Giacomelli's *Merope* (Venice, 1734), for example, included at least seven cadenzas![6]

Example 8-4. Telemann, first movement from the Sonata No. 2 in A major
(*Zwölf Methodische Sonaten*), with written-out ornamentation by the composer.

French ornamentation after 1660

Most ornamentation in French music is indicated with signs, although a few ornaments that could not be easily indicated with a sign were also used. Composers used different signs and even invented their own for some ornaments; thus each composer's marks must be interpreted independently. For this purpose, composers often included a table of ornament signs at the beginning of their editions. Despite the variety of signs in use, it is possible to approach French ornamentation by learning the characteristics of certain groups or families of ornaments. Even when a different sign is encountered, the ornament itself will therefore still be recognizable. Particularly valuable in this regard are two tables of ornaments by d'Anglebert (Table 8-1) and François Couperin (Table 8-2), which provide examples of the four main types of ornaments: (1) the appoggiatura, (2) the mordent, (3) fillers, and (4) articulations, or special effects.

The first group of ornaments, called the appoggiatura, or *port de voix*, consists of a dissonant note that is accented or stressed, held for a time, and resolved by step to a consonance. Its function is expressive, and its effect may vary from serious to graceful and light, depending upon the tempo and character of the piece. It is often combined with a dynamic stress such as a swell or diminuendo. The appoggiatura is usually held for at least half the value of the note it precedes. D'Anglebert demonstrates the rising and falling appoggiatura (Table 8-1, nos. 12 and 13), which he calls *cheute* or *port de voix*, and in each case the ornament is approached from the same direction in which it proceeds. Couperin indicates the appoggiatura with a small-size note (called a *petite note*) slurred to the note of resolution (Table 8-2, no. 5). Frequently the appoggiatura ends with a trill on its note of resolution. Couperin shows several trills, each beginning on the accented upper note, which is sometimes held as an appoggiatura (Table 8-2, nos. 6–10, 17).

The second group, called the mordent, or *pincé*, has a primarily rhythmic function rather than an expressive one. It is performed quickly and on the beat in order to achieve its function as an accent, and it may have one or more rapid beats to the lower auxiliary from a consonant written note. D'Anglebert illustrates the mordent (Table 8-1, nos. 9, 10, 29), and he also shows the trill with termination as a combination of the trill and mordent (Table 8-1, no. 11). Couperin illustrates the mordent as either *simple* (Table 8-2, no. 1) on a quarter note, or *double* (with more repercussions, Table 8-2, no. 2) on a half note, and even continuing on a very long note (Table 8-2, no. 16). It may be made more expressive by the addition of an appoggiatura (*port de voix*) from below, usually written as a small note slurred to the main note (Table 8-2, nos. 3 and 4).

The appoggiatura and mordent as two principal types of ornaments are encountered frequently in various contexts and combinations. An appoggiatura may take a prefix or suffix consisting of two or more notes which become part of the ornament (Table 8-1, nos. 5, 6, 11; Table 8-2, nos. 6, 7, 8). When the appoggiatura finishes with a trill, the speed may be varied according to the desired expressive quality. Low instruments and voices may use slower trills than higher voices or instruments, and the trill may gradually increase in speed.

Table 8-1. D'Anglebert's table of ornaments, from *Pièces de clavecin*, 1689.

Table 8-2. Francois Couperin's table of ornaments, from *Pièces de clavecin*, Book 1 (Paris, 1713).

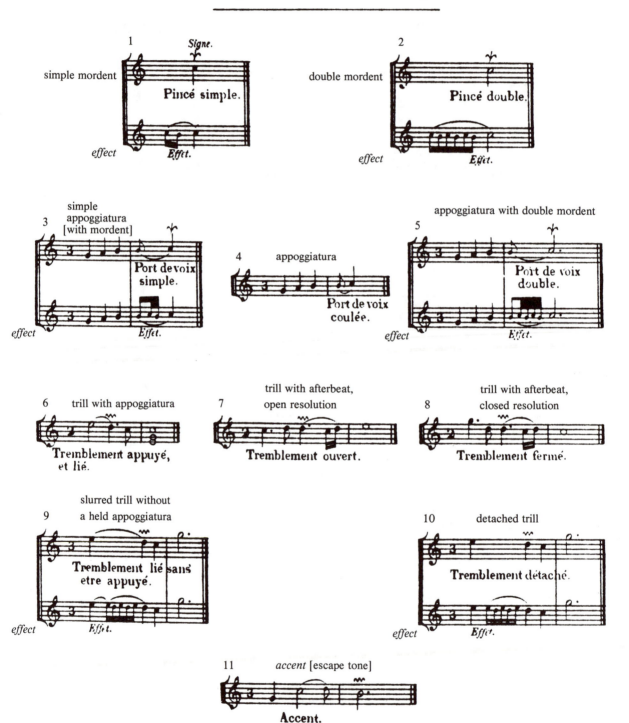

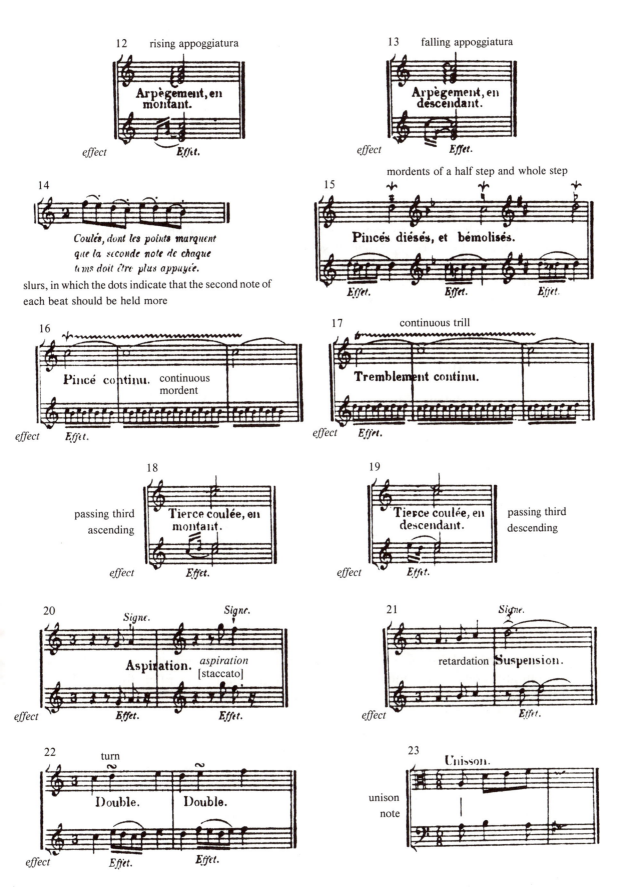

12   rising appoggiatura

13   falling appoggiatura

14

mordents of a half step and whole step

15

slurs, in which the dots indicate that the second note of
each beat should be held more

16   continuous mordent

17   continuous trill

18   passing third ascending

19   passing third descending

20

21   retardation

22   turn

23   unison note

A third category of ornament is the filler, which may consist of one or more notes that often fall between beats and are unaccented (Table 8-1, no. 18). Some may also occur on the beat, such as a slide from a third below the written pitch (Table 8-1, nos. 15–17, 19; Table 8-2, nos. 18, 19). Fillers may consist of nonchord tones that spread the notes of a chord, especially on a keyboard instrument, or of short, accented grace notes called *acciaccature* that are played as dissonances within a chord on the harpsichord, and are then released almost immediately. A frequently used type of filler in French music is the *tierce coulé*, an unaccented passing note between two notes a third apart, performed expressively and with a diminuendo. The filler may also consist of a group of notes, called a *tirade*, added between two notes, or of an anticipation played quickly before a consonant note.

The fourth type of ornament consists of various special effects and articulations, such as vibrato or *flattement*, a swell (also called *enflé*), or a slight delay, which Couperin calls *suspension* (Table 8-2, no. 21). The ornaments for special effect may be either expressive or primarily rhythmic in nature. The staccato which d'Anglebert indicates as no. 29 (Table 8-1) is the same as Couperin's *aspiration* (Table 8-2, no. 20).

Vocal ornamentation

The most detailed discussion of seventeenth-century vocal ornamentation is found in Bénigne de Bacilly's *Remarques curieuses sur l'art de bien chanter* (Paris, 1668). He describes ornaments appropriate for the *air de cour*, a courtly love song consisting of two stanzas for solo voice and accompaniment, in which written-out diminutions are frequently found in the second stanza. Other ornaments which Bacilly mentions that can be added by the singer are the appoggiatura (*port de voix*), trills (*cadence, double cadence*, and *demi-tremblement*), and dynamic nuances. He recommends the theorbo, harpsichord, and viol as appropriate instruments to accompany the voice, and suggests that the theorbo be played "with moderation" so that the voice can express the music and text freely.

The most important eighteenth-century French sources for vocal ornamentation are Jean Bérard's *L'art du chant* (Paris, 1755) and Michel Pignolet de Montéclair's *Principes de musique* (Paris, 1736). Montéclair describes eighteen ornaments in all, including appoggiaturas (the *port de voix* from below, and the *chûte* from above), the *coulé* or passing appoggiatura, five types of trill (with or without preparation), the mordent (*pincé*), turn (*tour de gosier*), fillers that may be slurred (*coulade*) or articulated (*trait*), vibrato (*flaté*), tremolo (*balancement*), and several dynamic nuances.

Several of the same ornaments (twelve in all) are described by Jean Bérard. He adds nineteen examples of airs and recitatives chosen from operatic works by Lully, Mondonville, Rameau, and others, in which he indicates with signs where each ornament may be added. In the more passionate airs, such as the monologue from Rameau's *Dardanus* entitled "Lieux funestes" (1744 version, act IV, scene 1), Bérard uses the *cadence molle* or soft trill (marked ✗), whose fluctuations are beaten slowly on the words "douleur" (sadness) and "déchirent" (from the verb "to tear"). The *son filé* (⅃) occurs on long notes, sometimes combined with the *accent* (T), a gentle upward inflection of pitch at the end of a note. For a simple, gavotte-like air such as "Votre coeur aimable" from Mondonville's *Titon et l'Aurore* (Example 8-5), he directs that the pronunciation should be marked with "sweetness and clarity," and he indicates primarily the *flaté* (vibrato ℇ) and appoggiatura, with a swell (*son filé* ⅃) on the highest note of the melody. Both Rameau and Mondonville indicated trills, but Bérard's examples are valuable for illustrating the different types of trill that might be appropriate and also for adding other nuances and ornaments that may not be indicated by the composer.

Example 8-5. (a) Mondonville, "Votre coeur aimable" from *Titon et l'Aurore*, and (b) with ornaments added by Bérard (*L'art du chant*, 1755).

Translation: Your heart, kind Aurora, is sensitive to my sighs. You love me, I adore you. Love gratifies our desires fully.

[Example 8-5. Continued]

(b) Bérard

For affected sounds
Exhale a little on each note, and execute the air with little
volume. Pronunciation should be marked by a sweetness and
extreme clarity, and the letters weakly [= barely] prepared.

J. S. Bach's ornamentation

Just as Bach's music shows an indebtedness to French, Italian, and north-German traditions, his ornamentation too belongs to several different styles which may even occur together in a single piece. Particularly noteworthy in his works is the use of many French signs for ornaments, some of which he illustrated in his table from the *Clavier-Büchlein* for Wilhelm Friedemann Bach (ca. 1720; Table 8-3). A comparison of this table with that of d'Anglebert demonstrates that each ornament is derived from one of those illustrated by d'Anglebert, or a combination of two or more of these. Bach's *trillo und mordant* (Table 8-3, no. 3), for example, is the same as d'Anglebert's *tremblement et pincé* (Table 8-1, no. 11). Likewise, Bach's *doppelt cadence und mordant* (Table 8-3, no. 7) is the same as d'Anglebert's *double cadence* combined with a *pincé* (Table 8-1, nos. 5 and 9).

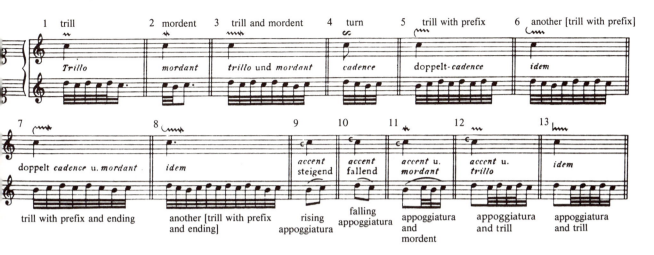

Table 8-3. J. S. Bach's table of ornaments from the *Clavier-Büchlein* for Wilhelm Friedemann Bach (ca. 1720).

In Bach's music, ornamentation may be indicated with French signs such as those illustrated in the foregoing table, but either French or Italian ornamentation may also be written out completely. His habit of prescribing his ornamentation exactly was criticised by Johann Adolph Scheibe, who observed in 1737 that "every ornament, every little grace, and everything that one thinks of as belonging to the method of playing, he expresses completely in notes."[7] The comment probably includes reference to articulation, bowing, and dynamics as well as ornaments that usually belong to the unwritten style or method of playing.

French ornamentation is most frequently found in suite movements whose musical and rhythmic character is also French, such as the courante, gavotte, sarabande, minuet, gigue, or bourée. Several sarabandes (nos. 2, 3, 6) in the English Suites (BWV 806–811)[8] have ornate *doubles*, although only no. 6 is so designated, and they feature numerous trills, appoggiaturas, mordents, *coulés*, and arpeggiations that recall the rich sonorities of the grand French sarabandes by Couperin. In the *double* of the sarabande from the third English Suite (Example 8-6), to which Bach gives the title "les agréments de la même Sarabande," trills, appoggiaturas, and long *tirades* or fillers decorate the melody, first in the right hand (mm. 1, 9) and later in the left hand (mm. 14, 21). Once recognized as such, the ornamentation may be shaped according to its direction and melodic function despite the notation in precise rhythmic values.

Italian ornamentation, sometimes mingled with some French signs, may be found in many of Bach's sonatas and arias. Among the more intricate examples of written-out ornamentation in the Italian style is the sinfonia from Cantata 21 ("Ich hatte viel Bekümmernis," Appendix A), in which the ornamented melodies of the oboe and violin are skillfully intertwined. There are also examples of Italian ornamentation in the adagio from the Sonata No. 3 in E for violin and harpsichord (BWV 1016), and the adagio from the unaccompanied Sonata No. 1 in B minor for violin (BWV 1014).[9]

Example 8-6. J. S. Bach, sarabande and *double* from the English Suite No. 3 (BWV 808).

Bach's technique of ornamenting a melody at the keyboard can be examined in the slow movements from the sixteen concertos transcribed for harpsichord in 1713 and 1714 from works by Vivaldi, Marcello, and others. In Concerto No. 2 (BWV 973),[10] transcribed from Vivaldi's Concerto in G (RV 332), the solo violin part in the second movement (largo cantabile) is written out by Bach in a fully ornamented fashion for harpsichord (Example 8-7a), and the string parts are adapted as a harmonic accompaniment in eighth notes. Bach's elaboration retains the melodic outline of Vivaldi's original (Example 8-7b), but he adds trills, mordants, and appoggiaturas as accents or to sustain longer notes, interspersed with passing notes and a few runs using a variety of different rhythms.

Ornamentation had a much greater significance than as mere decoration; it had an expressive role and thus was considered an obligatory part of an excellent performance. Perhaps the most intriguing aspect of the surviving evidence is that the performers who were most admired during the baroque era varied their rendition at every performance. For the modern singer or instrumentalist, learning to use ornamentation as an expressive vehicle and to vary it at will remains a significant challenge.

Bibliographical notes

For a list of some important treatises that discuss vocal and instrumental ornamentation, see Appendix C. Translations of the sections of Montéclair's treatise *Principes de musique Divisés en quatre parties* that deal with vocal ornamentation are included in the edition of Montéclair's cantatas by James R. Anthony and Diran Akmajian.

Example 8-7. a,b. J. S. Bach, *largo cantabile* from Concerto No. 2 (BWV 973), transcribed from Vivaldi's Concerto in G for violin, strings, and organ (RV 299).

On Caccini's expressive style of singing, see H. Wiley Hitchcock's article listed below, and his editions of Caccini's music with extensive commentary and the composer's prefaces (listed in Appendix C). Caccini's preface to the 1602 collection is also in *Strunk*, 377–392. Jane Glover's discussion of performance questions in Monteverdi's *Orfeo* is particularly helpful.

David Boyden and Hans Joachim Marx discuss the numerous surviving ornamented versions of Corelli's sonatas for violin and continuo. In an article on the French oboe in England, David Lasocki includes a slow movement by William Babell for violin or oboe and continuo with a plain version and ornaments by the composer similar to the type that might have been improvised in England about 1720. For further information on Bérard, see the preface to my edition of motets by François Martin; on both Bérard and Montéclair, see also the article by Nicholas McGegan and Gina Spagnoli.

Frederick Neumann contributes a valuable and extensive study in his *Ornamentation in Baroque and Post-Baroque Music*. Also useful is Neal Zaslaw's review of Neumann's book, which reexamines important issues raised by Neumann. Howard Ferguson surveys the main types of ornaments used in keyboard music. Particularly helpful are his discussion of ornamentation in English virginal music and a table of French ornaments used in keyboard music between 1670 and 1724.

FOR FURTHER STUDY

Boyden, David D. "Corelli's Solo Violin Sonatas 'Grac'd' by Dubourg." In *Festskrift Jens Peter Larsen*, 113–125. Copenhagen: Wilhelm Hansen, 1972.

_____ . "The Corelli 'Solo' Sonatas and Their Ornamental Additions by Corelli, Geminiani, Dubourg and the 'Walsh Anonymous'." In *Acta Scientifica* 3 (1972): 591–606.

Brown, Howard M. "Embellishing Eighteenth-Century Arias: on Cadenzas." In *Opera and Vivaldi*, ed. Michael Collins and Elise K. Kirk, 258–276. Austin: University of Texas Press, 1984.

Buelow, George J. "A Lesson in Operatic Performance by Madame Faustina Bordoni." In *A Musical Offering: Essays in Honor of Martin Bernstein*, ed. Edward H. Clinkscale and Claire Brook, 79–96. New York: Pendragon Press, 1977.

_____ . "Vocal Ornamentation in the Sacred Music of the Schütz Era." *American Choral Review* 24 no. 2–3 (1982): 5–13.

Caswell, Austin B. "Remarques curieuses sur l'art de bien chanter." *JAMS* 20 no. 1 (1967): 116–120.

Dean, Winton. *Three Ornamented Arias*. Oxford: Oxford University Press, 1976.

_____ . "Vocal embellishment in a Handel Aria." In *Studies in Eighteenth-Century Music: a Tribute to Karl Geiringer on his Seventieth Birthday*, ed. H. C. Robbins Landon and R. E. Chapman, 151–159. London: Allen & Unwin, 1970.

Ferguson, Howard. *Keyboard Interpretation from the 14th to the 19th Century*. New York and London: Oxford University Press, 1975.

Glover, Jane. "Recreating 'Orfeo' for the Modern Stage: Solving the Musical Problems." In *Claudio Monteverdi: Orfeo*, ed. John Whenham, 138–155. Cambridge: Cambridge University Press, 1986.

Hitchcock, H. Wiley. "Vocal Ornamentation in Caccini's *Nuove Musiche*." *MQ* 56 (1970): 389–404.

Jones, Edward Huws. *The Performance of English Song, 1610–1670*. New York: Garland, 1989.

Lasocki, David. "The French Hautboy in England, 1673–1730." *EM* 16 (1988): 339–357.

Martin, François. *Motets for One and Two Voices with Instruments*. Recent Researches in Music of the Classical Era, v. 29, ed. Mary Cyr. Madison: A-R Editions, 1988.

Marx, Hans Joachim. "Some Unknown Embellishments of Corelli's Violin Sonatas." *MQ* 61 (1975): 65–76.

McGegan, Nicholas and Gina Spagnoli. "Singing Style at the Opéra in the Rameau Period." In *Jean-Philippe Rameau colloque international organisé par la société Rameau, Dijon 21–24 septembre 1983*, ed. Jérome de la Gorce, 209–226. Paris: Champion, 1987.

Neumann, Frederick. *Ornamentation in Baroque and Post-Baroque Music, with Special Emphasis on J. S. Bach*. Princeton: Princeton University Press, 1978.

O'Donnell, John. "Bach's Trills: Some Historical and Contextual Considerations." *Musicology* [Journal of the Musicological Society of Australia] 4 (1974): 14–24.

Zaslaw, Neal. "Baroque Ornamentation [review of Neumann's book]." *EM* 9 (January 1981): 63–68.

NOTES TO CHAPTER 8

1. For examples, see the articles by Brown and Buelow in the bibliography at the end of this chapter. An ornamented aria is also included in Hellmuth Christian Wolff, *Original Vocal Improvisations from the Sixteenth-Eighteenth Centuries*, transl. A. C. Howie (Cologne: A. Volk Verlag, 1972), 143–168.
2. *MonteverdiW*, v. 8, part 2, p. 314.
3. Facs. in *L'Orfeo favola in musica* (Venice, 1615), introduction by Denis Stevens (Amersham, England: Gregg International Publishers Ltd., 1972); modern edition in *MonteverdiW*, v. 11.
4. The edition of Corelli's violin sonatas (Op. 5) edited by Joachim and Chrysander includes the ornamented versions of the slow movements. Geminiani's ornaments for Op. 5, No. 9 are in John Hawkins, *A General History of the Science and Practice of Music* (1776), R of London, 1853 ed. (New York: Dover Publications, 1963), v. 2, p. 848f. See also the articles by Boyden, Marx, and Zaslaw in the bibliography at the end of this chapter.
5. Telemann, *Zwölf Methodische Sonaten*, ed. Max Seiffert, 2 v. (Kassel: Bärenreiter, 1965).
6. Examples of cadenzas sung by Faustina and Farinelli can be found in Brown, "Embellishing Eighteenth-Century Arias," 261–263.
7. Johann Adolph Scheibe, "letter from an able *Musikant* abroad" dated May 14, 1737, in *The Bach Reader*, ed. Hans T. David and Arthur Mendel (New York: Norton, 1966), 238.
8. J. S. Bach, *NBA*, ser. 5, v. 7.
9. J. S. Bach, *NBA*, ser. 6, v. 1.
10. J. S. Bach, *NBA*, ser. 5, v. 11.

Appendix A:
Guide to Scores

A companion audio cassette contains the recordings recommended below. To order, please write to Amadeus Press, 9999 S.W. Wilshire, Suite 124, Portland, OR 97225, U.S.A.

Johann Sebastian Bach

Cantata No. 8

Recitative ("Zwar fühlt mein schwaches Herz") and aria ("Doch weichet, ihr tollen") from *Liebster Gott, wenn werd ich sterben* (BWV 8)

For discussion, see pp. 54, 77.

Score: *BGA*. R (Amersham, Bucks, England: Gregg Press International: 1968), 1: 229–240.

Recording: Johann Sebastian Bach, *Cantatas BWV 8, 78, 99*, The Bach Ensemble, directed by Joshua Rifkin. Allan Fast, countertenor; Jan Opalach, bass. Decca (London) 421 728–2. Courtesy of Polygram Records of Canada, Inc.

Text translation

(Recitative)

It is true that my feeble heart feels
   fear, sorrow, pain;
   where will my body find repose?
Who then will free and unbind my soul
   from its yoke of sin?
My goods will be scattered;
   and where will my loved ones
   in their sadness
   be scattered and driven?

(Aria)

Away, you extravagant, vain thoughts!
My Jesus calls me; who would not go?
Nothing that is agreeable to me
   is found in this world.
Appear to me, blessed, cheerful morning;
   radiant and glorious, I stand before Jesus.

Johann Sebastian Bach

Sinfonia from Cantata No. 21

Sinfonia from *Ich hatte viel Bekümmernis* (BWV 21)

For discussion, see p. 139.

Score: *BGA*. R (Amersham, Bucks, England: Gregg Press International, 1968), 5/1: 1–3.

Recording: *Das Kantatenwerk*, vol. 6. Concentus Musicus Wien. Nikolaus Harnoncourt, Musical Direction. Teldec 242502–2 (1973). The master recording was re-recorded with the permission of Teldec Classics International GmbH.

Dieterich Buxtehude

Sonata for violin, viola da gamba, and harpsichord

Sonata in A, Op. 2, No. 5 (1696)
For discussion, see pp. 37–38, 120.
Score: *DDT*, ed. Carl Stiehl and Hans Joachim Moser (Wiesbaden: Breitkopf & Härtel, 1957), 11: 126–138.
Recording: Buxtehude, *Alto Cantatas and Sonatas*; Sophie Rivard, baroque violin; Mary Cyr, viola da gamba; Sandra Mangsen, harpsichord. McGill Records 750031–2 (1988).

Da capo
se piace.

André Campra

Forlana

Forlana from *L'Europe galante* (1697)

For discussion, see pp. 25–26.

Score: *L'Europe galante* (Paris, 1724). R (Amersham, Bucks, England: Gregg Press International: 1967), 191–194.

Recording: Campra, *L'Europe galante*. La petite bande; Sigiswald Kuijken, concertmaster; Gustav Leonhardt, director. Deutsche Harmonia Mundi 77059-2-RG (1988).

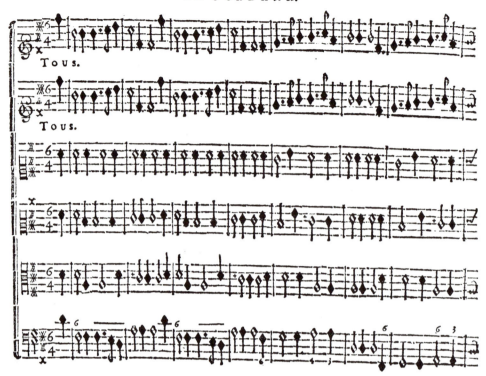

L'EUROPE GALANTE, BALLET.

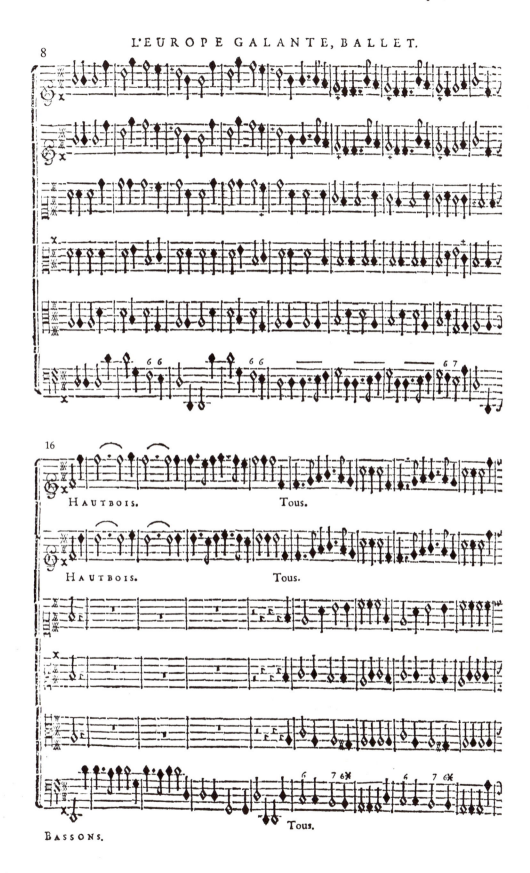

QUATRIE'ME ENTRE'E, SCENE II.

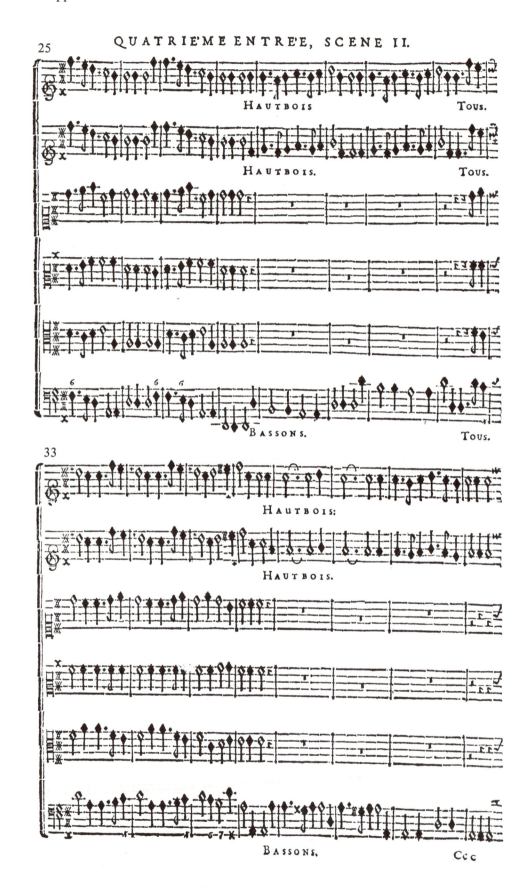

L'EUROPE GALANTE, BALLET.

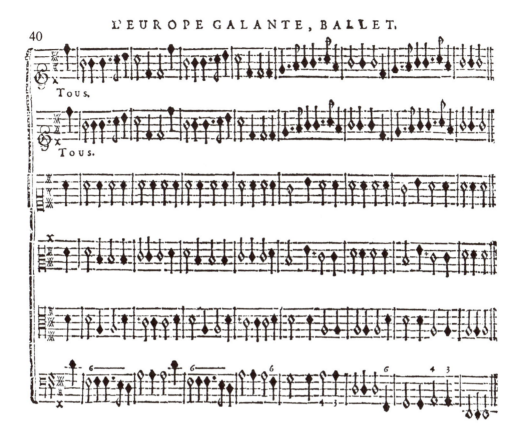

Arcangelo Corelli

Sonata for violin and basso continuo

Sonata Op. 5, No. 5

For discussion, see pp. 40, 51, 119, 129.

Score: *Sonate a violino e violone o cimbalo* (Amsterdam, 1710). R (Florence: Studio per edizione scelte, 1979), 42–51.

Recording: Corelli, *Violin Sonatas, Op. 5*. Trio Sonnerie: Monica Huggett, violin; Mitzi Meyerson, harpsichord, organ; Sarah Cunningham, cello; Nigel North, archlute, theorbo. Virgin Classics VCD 790840–2 (1990).

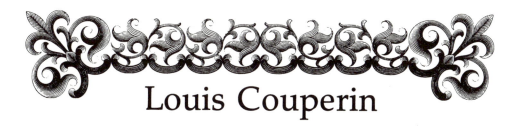

Louis Couperin

Unmeasured prelude

Prelude in F for harpsichord

For discussion, see pp. 61, 110.

Scores: (a) Modern edition, ed. Mary Cyr. (b) Facsimile of the Bauyn
manuscript. Paris, Bibliothèque Nationale, Réserve Vm⁷674–
675, ff. 17–18. In *Manuscrit Bauyn: Pièces de clavecin c. 1660*
(Geneva: Minkoff, 1977), 169–171.

Recording: L. Couperin, *Intégrale de l'oeuvre de clavecin*. Davitt
Moroney, harpsichord. Harmonia mundi (France) HMA
1901124.27 (1983; CD 1989).

(a)

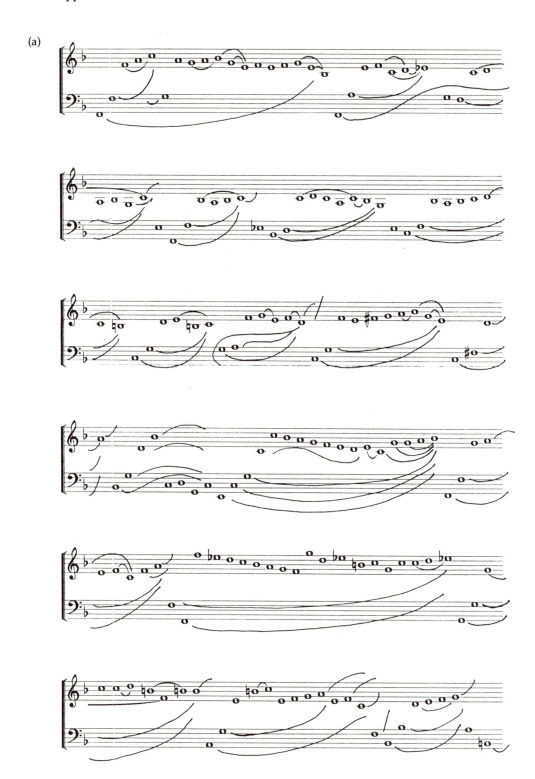

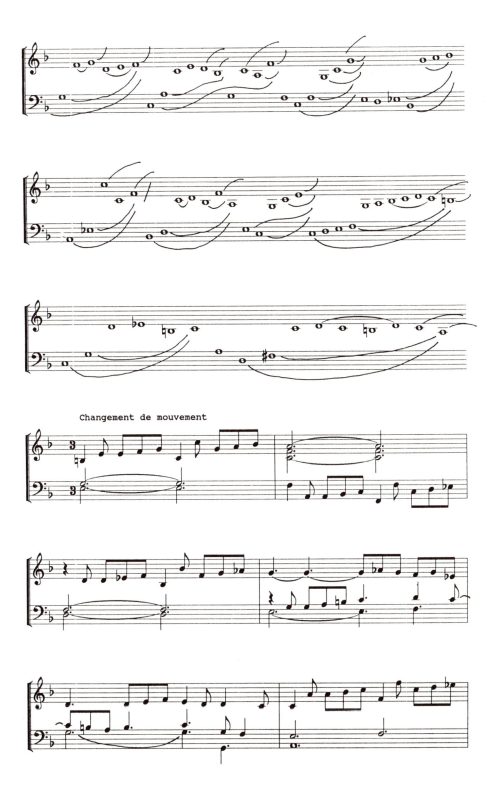

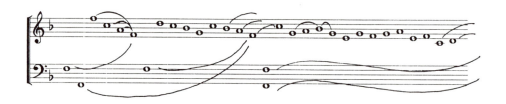

(b)

Suitte

George Friderich Handel

Aria from *Flavio*

"Sirti, scogli, tempeste," from *Flavio* (Act III, scene 3)
For discussion, see pp. 35–36, 61, 130.
Score: *HandelW*, 21: 70–72. R (Amersham, Bucks, England: Gregg
    Press International, 1965), 21: 70–72.
Recording: Handel, *Flavio*. Ensemble 415, directed by René Jacobs.
    Christina Högman, soprano. Harmonia Mundi (France)
    901312.13 (1990).

Text translation

VITIGE:

Sandbanks, rocks, tempests, storms
    are what the stars point to
    in the sea of love.
So bitter are my woes that,
    uncertain whether there is hope,
    grief is a burden to me.

Jean-Baptiste Lully

Ouverture to
Le bourgeois gentilhomme

Ouverture to *Le bourgeois gentilhomme* (1670)
For discusssion, see pp. 92–93.
Score: *Oeuvres complètes de J.-B. Lully*, ed. Henry Prunières (Paris: Editions de la Revue Musicale, 1938), 3: 43–46.
Recording: Lully, *Le bourgeois gentilhomme*. La petite bande; Sigiswald Kuijken, concertmaster; Gustav Leonhardt, director. Deutsche Harmonia Mundi 77059–2-RG (1988).

OUVERTURE

Text translation

ORPHEUS:

Powerful spirit and formidable deity,
   without whom the soul separated from its
   body cannot hope to gain passage to the other shore,

I am not living, no, because since my dear
   spouse is departed, my heart is no longer with me,
   and without a heart, how would I be able to live?

Toward her I have made my way through the murky air,
   and have not gone to Hades, for wherever such
   beauty is found, paradise must be.

I am Orpheus, who follows Eurydice's steps
   through these shadowy dunes,
   where no mortal man has ever gone.

O serene light of lights,
   if one glance from you can bring me back to life,
   alas, who would deny comfort to my troubles?

Only you, noble god, can come to my aid,
   and fear not, because on a golden lyre,
   I arm my fingers with sweet strings
   against which the most rigid soul yields to their power.

Claudio Monteverdi

Aria from *Orfeo*

"Possente spirto," from *Orfeo* (1609)

For discussion, see pp. 73, 111, 127–128.

Score: *MonteverdiW*. R (Vienna, Austria: n.d.), 11: 84–102. Ed. Francesco Malipiero. Copyright by Universal Edition, Vienna. All rights reserved. Used by permission of European American Music Distributors Corporation, sole United States and Canadian agent for Universal Edition, Vienna.

Recording: Monteverdi, *L'Orfeo*. Nikolaus Harnoncourt, conductor. Lajos Kozma, Orfeo. The Capella antiqua München, conducted by Konrad Ruhland. The Concentus Musicus Wien. Das Alte Werk (Teldec) 8.35020 ZA (1985). The master recording was re-recorded with the permission of Teldec Classics International GmbH.

Orpheus sings only one of the two parts to the sound of an organ with wooden pipes and a chitarrone.

Orfeo al suono del organo di legno, e un chitarrone canta una sola de le due parti.

Ritornello

Ritornello

1) A questo punto finisce la variazione: le due parti si riuniscono.
At this point, the variations finish; the two lines are united.

Furno sonate le altre parti da tre Viole da braccio, et un contrabasso de Viola tocchi pian piano.

The three upper parts are played by three viole da braccio, *and a violone plays [the bass line] softly.*

Jean-Philippe Rameau

Menuet for harpsichord

Menuet in G
For discussion, see p. 118.
Score: *Nouvelles suites de pièces de clavecin* (Paris, 1728). R (New York:
Broude Brothers, 1967), 20.
Recording: Rameau, *Nouvelles Suites de Pièces de Clavecin (1728)*.
William Christie, harpsichord. Harmonia Mundi (France)
HMC 901121 (1987).

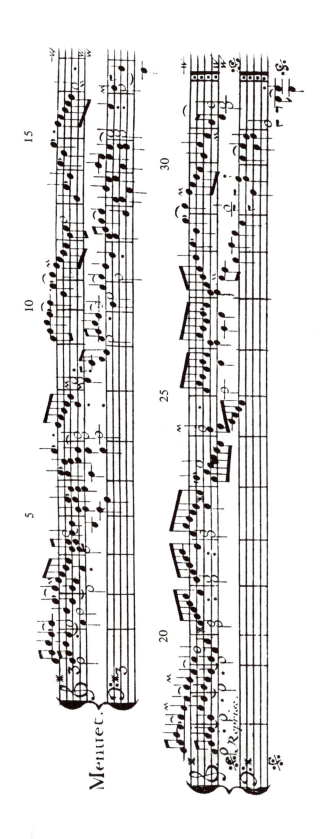

Jean-Philippe Rameau

Menuet and air
from *Castor et Pollux*

Menuet and air, "Naissez dons de Flore," from the prologue to *Castor et Pollux* (1737)

For discussion, see p. 118.

Score: Rameau, *Castor et Pollux* (Paris, 1737), 27 and 29–32. From the copy in the Music Library, University of California, Berkeley.

Recording: Rameau, *Castor et Pollux*. Concentus Musicus Wien; Nikolaus Harnoncourt, Musical Direction; Stockholmer Kammerchor; Eric Ericson, Conductor. Zeger Vandersteene, L'Amour. Das Alte Werk 8.35048ZB (1972). The master recording was re-recorded with the permission of Teldec Classics International GmbH.

Text translation

LOVE:

Arise, gifts of Flora,
   peace must revive you,
   arise, it's time to blossom forth;
   for us, it's the time to love.

CHORUS:
Arise, gifts of Flora, *etc.*

LOVE:

Young Zephyr,
Fly and escape pleasure!
Pour out flowers!
Hearts at every moment make
   the most charming knots.
Let us lend our wings to the beauties,
   to make more lovers happy.

CHORUS:
Young Zephyr, *etc.*

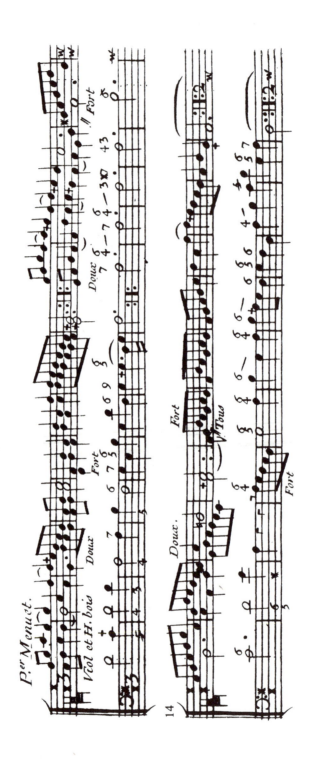

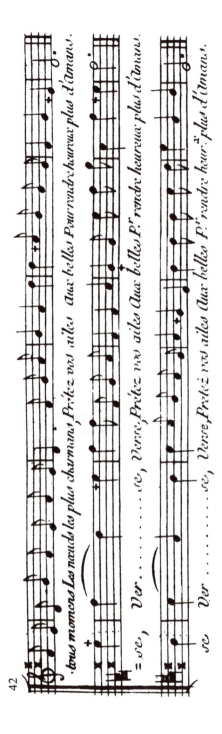

Appendix B:
Bibliographies and
General Studies
of Performance Practice

Brown, Howard Mayer, and Stanley Sadie, eds. *Performance Practice: Music after 1600.* The New Grove Handbooks in Music. New York and London: W. W. Norton and Co., 1989.

Damschroder, David, and David Russell Williams. *Music Theory from Zarlino to Schenker: a Bibliography and Guide.* 2 v. Stuyvesant, New York: Pendragon, 1989.

Dart, Thurston. *The Interpretation of Music.* New York: Harper and Row, 1954, 1963.

Dolmetsch, Arnold. *The Interpretation of the Music of the XVIIth and XVIIIth Centuries.* London: Novello, 1915.

Donington, Robert. *A Performer's Guide to Baroque Music.* New York: Charles Scribner's Sons, 1973.

_____ . *Baroque Music: Style and Performance.* London: Faber Music, 1982.

_____ . *The Interpretation of Early Music. New Version.* London: Faber and Faber, 1989.

_____ . *String Playing in Baroque Music.* London: Charles Scribner's Sons, 1976.

Ferand, Ernest T. *Die Improvisation in Beispielen aus neun Jahrhunderten abendländischer Musik.* Cologne: Arno Volk Verlag, 1956.

Frotscher, Gotthold. *Aufführungspraxis alter Musik.* Wilhelmshaven, Amsterdam: Heinrichshofen, 1963. Transl. Kurt Michaelis as *Performing Practices of Early Music: a Comprehensive Reference Work about Music of Past Ages for Musicians, Interpreters, and Amateurs.* New York: Heinrichshofen Edition, 1981.

Geoffrey-Dechaume, A. *Les 'secrets' de la musique ancienne.* Paris: Fasquelle, 1964.

Harnoncourt, Nikolaus. *Der Musikalische Dialog. Gedanken zu Monteverdi, Bach und Mozart.* Salzburg and Vienna: Residenz Verlag, 1984. Transl. Dennis Collins as *Le dialogue musical Monteverdi, Bach, et Mozart.* [Paris]: Editions Gallimard, 1985. Transl. Mary O'Neill as *The Musical Dialogue: Thoughts on Monteverdi, Bach, and Mozart.* Portland, OR: Amadeus Press, 1989.

_____ . *Musik als Klangrede Wege zu einem neuen Musikverständnis.* Salzburg and Vienna: Residenz Verlag, 1982. Transl. Dennis Collins as *Le discours musical: pour une*

241

nouvelle conception de la musique. [Paris]: Editions Gallimard, 1988. Transl. Mary O'Neill as *Baroque Music Today: Music as Speech, Ways to a New Understanding of Music*. Portland, OR: Amadeus Press, 1988.

Jackson, Roland. *Performance Practice, Medieval to Contemporary: a Bibliographical Guide*. New York: Garland, 1988.

le Huray, Peter. *Authenticity in Performance: Eighteenth-Century Case Studies*. Cambridge: Cambridge UP, 1990.

MacClintock, Carol, ed. *Readings in the History of Music in Performance*. Bloomington: Indiana University Press, 1979.

Neumann, Frederick. *Essays in Performance Practice*. UMI Studies in Musicology, no. 58. Ann Arbor: UMI Research Press, 1982.

_____ . *New Essays on Performance Practice*. Ann Arbor: UMI Research Press, 1989.

"Performance Practice Bibliography." In *Performance Practice Review* 2 (Fall 1989), 178–239.

Powell, Newman Wilson. *Rhythmic Freedom in the Performance of French Music from 1650 to 1735*. PhD diss., Stanford University, 1958.

Rangel-Ribeiro, Victor. *Baroque Music, a Practical Guide for the Performer*. New York: Schirmer, 1981.

Rowen, Ruth Halle. *Music through Sources and Documents*. New Jersey: Prentice-Hall, 1979.

Schmitz, Hans-Peter. *Die Kunst der Verzierung im 18. Jahrhundert*. Kassel: Bärenreiter, 1965.

Strunk, Oliver, ed. *Source Readings in Music History from Classical Antiquity through the Romantic Era*. New York: Norton, 1950.

Veilhan, Jean-Claude, *Les règles de l'interprétation musicale à l'époque baroque (XVIIe-XVIIIe siècles), générales à tous les instruments*. Paris: A. Leduc, 1977. Transl. John Lambert as *The Rules of Musical Interpretation in the Baroque Era*. Paris: A. Leduc, 1979.

Vinquist, Mary, and Neal Zaslaw, "Performance Practice: a Bibliography," *Current Musicology* 8 (1969), 10 (1970); supplements 12 (1971) and 15 (1973), also published separately (New York: W. W. Norton and Co., 1971).

Weiss, Piero, and Richard Taruskin. *Music in the Western World: a History in Documents*. New York: Schirmer, 1984.

Westrup, Jack. *Musical Interpretation*. London: British Broadcasting Corporation, 1971.

Appendix C:
Pre-1800 Sources Cited

Adlung, Jacob. *Anleitung zu der musikalischen Gelahrtheit*. Erfurt, 1758. Facs. ed. Hans Joachim Moser. Kassel: Bärenreiter, 1953.

_____ . *Musica mechanica organoedi* (ca. 1726). Ed. Johann Lorenz Albrecht, with additions by Johann Friedrich Agricola. Berlin, 1768. Facs. 2 v., Kassel: Bärenreiter, 1931. Partial trans. Ross Wesley Ellison as "Baroque Organ Registration: Chapter Eight of Jacob Adlung's *Musica mechanica organoedi* 1768." *Music* [A.G.O. and R.C.C.O. Magazine] 8 (1974) 25–28, 50–51.

Agazzari, Agostino. *Del sonare sopra'l basso con tutti stromenti & dell'uso loro nel conserto*. Siena, 1607. (In *Strunk*, "Of Playing upon a Bass with All Instruments and of Their Use in the Consort," 424–431. Also in *MacClintock*, 130–133.)

Agricola, Johann Friedrich. *Anleitung zur Singkunst*. Berlin, 1757. [A German translation of Tosi's *Opinioni* (Bologna, 1723) with additions.] R Celle: Moeck, 1966.

Anglebert, Jean-Henri d'. "Principes de l'accompagnment." In *Pièces de clavecin* (Paris, 1689), ed. Kenneth Gilbert. Paris: Heugel, 1975.

Bach, Carl Philipp Emanuel. *Versuch über die wahre Art das Clavier zu spielen*. Berlin, 1753; part 2, 1762. Transl. W. J. Mitchell as *Essay on the True Art of Playing Keyboard Instruments*. New York: Norton, 1949. (For excerpt, see *MacClintock*, 305–316.)

Bacilly, Bénigne de. *Remarques curieuses sur l'art de bien chanter*. Paris, 1668. R (1679 ed.) Geneva: Minkoff, 1971. Transl. Austin B. Caswell as *A Commentary upon the Art of Proper Singing*. New York: Institute of Mediaeval Music, 1968.

Bassano, Giovanni. *Ricercate, passaggi et cadentie*. Venice, 1585. R Zurich: Pelikan, 1976.

Bérard, Jean. *L'art du chant*. Paris, 1755. R Geneva: Minkoff, 1972. Transl. Sidney Murray as *Jean Bérard's 'L'art du chant': Translation and Commentary*. Milwaukee: Pro Musica Press, 1969.

Blow, John. Treatise on playing from a "Through'-Bass." Manuscript, London, British Library Additional 34072, ff. 1–5.

Bonnet[-Bourdelot], Jacques. *Histoire de la musique et de ses effets*. 4 v. Paris, 1715. R 1969. (For excerpt, see *MacClintock*, 240–250.)

Bremner, Robert. *Thoughts on the Performance of Concert Music* [preface to Six Quartettos by J. G. Schetky]. London, 1777. R London: H. Baron, 1972.

Brossard, Sebastian de. *Dictionaire (sic) de musique contenant une explication des termes grecs, latins, italiens, & françois les plus usitez . . .* Paris, 1703. Second edition, Paris, 1705. R of 1703 edition Amsterdam: Antiqua, 1964. R Hilversum: Frits Knuf, 1965. Transl. Albion Gruber as *Dicitonary of Music*. Music Theorists in Translation, v. 12. Henryville: Institute of Mediaeval Music, 1982.

Brosses, Charles de, *Lettres historiques et critique sur l'Italie*. Paris, 1799. *Le président de Brosses en Italie: lettres familières écrites d'Italie en 1739 et 1740*. Third ed. Paris: P. Didier and Co., 1869. *Lettre d'Italie sur les spectacles et la musique. Lettres d'Italie du Président de Brosses*. 2 v. Ed. Frédéric d'Agay. Paris: Mercure de France, 1986. (For excerpt, see *MacClintock*, 268–287.)

Burney, Charles. *The Present State of Music in France and Italy*. London, 1771. R (1773 and 1775 ed.) New York: Broude Brothers, 1969. (For excerpt, see *Rowen*, 218–221.)

Caccini, Giulio. *Le Nuove Musiche*. Florence, 1601[1602]. R New York: Broude Brothers, 1987. Modern edition ed. H. Wiley Hitchcock. Recent Researches in the Music of the Baroque Era, v. 9. Madison: A-R Editions, 1970. Preface transl. into English in John Playford's *Introduction to the Skill of Music*. Fourth-Twelfth editions (First ed., London, 1653). R (Twelfth ed., 1694) New York: Da Capo Press, 1972. (Preface also in *Strunk*, 377–392. For excerpt, see *Rowen*, 149–150.)

_____. *Nuove musiche e nuova maniera di scriverle*. Florence, 1614. R Florence: Studio per Edizioni Scelte, 1983. Modern edition ed. H. Wiley Hitchcock. Recent Researches in Music of the Baroque Era, v. 28. Madison: A-R Editions, 1978.

Casa, Girolamo dalla. *Il vero modo di diminuir, libro secundo*. Venice, 1584.

Charpentier, Marc-Antoine. *Règles de composition* (ca. 1682). Manuscript, Paris, Bibliothèque Nationale, nouv. acq. 6355.

Corrette, Michel. *L'école d'Orphée*. Paris, 1738. R Geneva: Minkoff, 1972.

_____. *Le maître de clavecin pour l'accompagnement, méthode théorique et pratique*. Paris, 1753. R Bologna: Arnaldo Forni, 1969; Hildesheim: Georg Olms, 1973. Geneva: Minkoff, 1976; New York: Broude Brothers, 1976.

_____. *Méthode raisonnée pour apprendre à jouer de la flûte traversiere*. Paris and Lyon, (ca. 1740). R Buren, The Netherlands: Frits Knuf, 1978; Geneva: Minkoff, 1978. Transl. Carol Reglin Farrar as *Michel Corrette and Flute-Playing in the Eighteenth Century*. New York: Institute of Mediaeval Music, 1970.

_____. *Prototipes contenant des leçons d'accompagnement pour servir d'addition au livre intitulé le maître de clavecin*. Paris, 1775. R Geneva: Minkoff, 1976.

Couperin, François. *L'art de toucher le clavecin*. Paris, 1716. R New York: Broude Brothers, 1969. Transl. Margery Halford as *The Art of Playing the Harpsichord*. New York: Alfred Publishers, 1974. (For excerpts, see *MacClintock*, 224–229 and *Rowen*, 186–188.)

Dandrieu, Jean François. *Principes de l'accompagnement du clavecin*. Paris, 1718. R Geneva: Minkoff, 1972.

Delair, Denis. *Traité de l'accompagnement sur le théorbe et le clavecin*. Paris, 1690. Geneva: Minkoff, 1972.

DeMachy, [?]. *Pièces de violle*. Paris, 1685. R Geneva: Minkoff, 1973.

Diruta, Girolamo. *Il transilvano*. Part 1: Venice, 1593; part 2: Venice, 1609. R Ed. Giuseppe Vecchi, Bibliotheca musica Bononiensis, series 2, no. 132, Bologna: Forni, [1969]. (For excerpt, see *MacClintock*, 87–95.)

Fantini, Girolama. *Modo per imparare a sonare di tromba*. Frankfurt, 1638; R Nashville: The Brass Press, 1972. Transl. Edward H. Tarr as *Method for Learning to Play the Trumpet . . .* Nashville: The Brass Press, 1975.

Freillon-Poncein, Jean Pierre. *La véritable manière d'apprendre à jouer en perfection du hautbois, de la flûte et du flageolet*. Paris, 1700. R Geneva: Minkoff, 1974.

Gaffurius, Franchinus. *Pratica musicae*. Milan, 1496. Transl. Clement A. Miller, Dallas: American Institute of Musicology, 1968. Transl. Irwin Young, Madison: University of Wisconsin Press, 1969.

Gasparini, Francesco. *L'armonico pratico al cimbalo*. Venice, 1708. Transl. F. S. Stillings and ed. D. L. Burrows, as *The Practical Harmonist at the Harpsichord*. New Haven: Yale School of Music, 1963. R New York: Da Capo, 1980. R New York: Broude, 1967.

Geminiani, Francesco. *A Treatise of Good Taste in the Art of Musick*. London, 1749 R New York: Da Capo, 1969.

———. *The Art of Playing on the Violin*. London, 1751. Facs., introduction by David Boyden, London: Oxford University Press, 1952. (For excerpt, see *MacClintock*, 293–297.)

Gervais, [Laurent]. *Méthode pour l'accompagnement du clavecin*. Paris, [1733].

Hawkins, John. *A General History of the Science and Practice of Music* (London, 1776). R (London, 1843 ed.) 2 v. New York: Dover Publications, 1963.

Heinichen, *Der General-Bass in der Composition* (Dresden, 1728). R 1969. Partial transl. (the *Einleitung*) George J. Buelow, *Thorough-Bass Accompaniment according to Johann David Heinichen*. Revised ed. Ann Arbor: UMI Research Press, 1986.

Hotteterre le Romain, Jacques. *L'art de préluder sur la flûte traversière, sur la flûte-à-bec, sur le hautbois et autres instruments de dessus*. Op. 7. Paris, 1719. R Paris: A. Zurfluh, 1966.

———. *Principes de la flûte traversière, ou flûte d'Allemagne, de la flûte à bec, ou flûte douce, et du haut-bois*. Paris, 1707. Facs. of 1728 edition ed. H. H. Hellwig. Kassel: Bärenreiter, 1958. Transl. David Lasocki as *Principles of the Flute, Recorder, and Oboe*. New York: Praeger, 1968.

Kirnberger, Johann Philipp. *Die Kunst des reinen Satzes in der Musik*. Berlin, 1771. R (1776 ed.) Hildesheim: Georg Olms, 1968. Transl. David Beach and Jürgen Thym as *The Art of Strict Musical Composition by Johann Philipp Kirnberger*. New Haven: Yale University Press, 1982. (For excerpt, see *Rowen*, 212–218.)

LaBorde, Jean Benjamin de. *Essai sur la musique ancienne et moderne*. 4 vols. Paris, 1780. R New York, AMS Press, 1978.

Locke, Matthew. *Melothesia or Certain General Rules for Playing upon a Continued-Bass*. London, 1673. R New York: Broude Brothers, 1975.

Mably, Bonnot de. *Lettres à Madame la Marquise de P . . . sur l'opéra*. Paris, 1741.

Mace, Thomas. *Musick's Monument*. London, 1676. Paris: Editions du Centre Nationale de la Recherche Scientifique, 1958–1966.

Mahaut, Anton. *Nouvelle méthode pour apprendre en peu de temps à jouer de la flûte traversière*. Paris, 1759. R Geneva: Minkoff, 1972.

Mancini, Giambattista. *Pensieri, e reflessioni pratiche sopra il canto figurato*. Vienna, 1774. R Bologna: Forni, 1970. Transl. Edward Foreman as *Practical Reflections on Figured Singing*. Champaign, IL: Pro Musica Press, 1967.

Marais, Marin. *Pièces de violes 2ᵉ livre*. Paris, 1701. R Basel: R. Ebner, 1978. Ed. John Hsu. New York: Broude Trust, 1986.

———. *Pièces de violes 3ᵉ livre*. Paris, 1711. R Basel: R. Ebner, 1979.

Mattheson, Johann. *Das neu-eröffnete Orchestre*. Hamburg, 1713.

———. *Der volkommene Capellmeister*. Hamburg, 1739. Facs. ed. Margarete Reimann. Kassel: Bärenreiter, 1954. Transl. Ernest C. Harriss. UMI Studies in Musicology no. 21. UMI Research Press: Ann Arbor, 1981.

Mersenne, Marin. *Harmonie universelle*. Paris, 1636. Facs. in 3 v. ed. François Lesure. Paris: Editions du centre national de la recherche scientifique, 1965. Transl. Roger E. Chapman as *Harmonie universelle: The Books on Instruments*. The Hague: Martinus Nijhoff, 1957 R 1964.

Montéclair, Michel Pignolet de. *Principes de musique divisés en quatre parties*. Paris, 1736. R Geneva: Minkoff, 1972.

Monteverdi, Claudio. *Madrigali guerrieri ed amorosi*. Venice, 1638. (Foreword in *Strunk*, 413–415.)

Mozart, Leopold. *Versuch einer gründlichen Violinschule*. Augsburg, 1756. R Vienna: Carl Stephenson, [1922]. Transl. Edith Knocker as *A Treatise on the Fundamental Principles of Violin Playing*. Second ed. Oxford: Oxford University Press, 1951; R 1985.

Muffat, Georg. *Florilegium primum*. Augsburg, 1695. In *DTÖ*, series 2, v. 4. Preface ed. Walter Kolneder as *Georg Muffat zur Aufführungspraxis* (in French, German, Italian, and Latin). Second ed. Baden-Baden: Koerner, 1990. (For excerpt of preface, see *MacClintock*, 297–303 and *Strunk*, 442–445.)

———. *Florilegium secundum*. Passau, 1698. Preface in *Strunk*, 445–448. Preface ed. Kolneder [see under Muffat's *Florilegium primum*].

Niedt, Friedrich Erhard. *Musicalische Handleitung*. Hamburg, 1700. R Buren, The Netherlands: Frits Knuf, 1976. Transl. Pamela L. Poulin as *The Musical Guide*. New York: Oxford University Press, 1988. (Foreword in *Strunk*, 463–470.)

Pasquali, Nicolo. *Thorough-Bass Made Easy*. Edinburgh, 1757. Facs. ed. John Churchill. London: Oxford University Press, 1974.

Playford, John. *An Introduction to the Skill of Musick*. London, 1654. Facs. of twelfth ed. (London, 1694) New York: Da Capo, 1972.

Praetorius, Michael. *De organographia*. v. 2 of *Syntagma musicum*. Wolfenbüttel, 1619. Facs. R Kassel: Bärenreiter, 1958. [Modern transcription:] Publikation aelterer praktischer und theoretischer Musikwerke, v. 13, New York: Broude, 1966. Transl. Harold Blumenfeld as *The 'Syntagma musicum' of Michael Praetorius, Volume Two: 'De organographia,' First and Second Parts*. New York: Bärenreiter, 1962; R New York: Da Capo, 1980. (For excerpts, see *MacClintock*, 142–149 and *Rowen*, 141–148.)

Prelleur, Peter. *The Modern Musik-Master or, the Universal Musician*. London, 1731. R Kassel: Bärenreiter, 1965.

Purcell, Henry. *Twelve Sonatas of 3 Parts*. London, 1683. Ed. J. A. Fuller Maitland [preface in facs.]. London: Novello, Ewer and Co., 1893. (Preface in *Rowen*, 176–178.)

Quantz, Johann Joachim. *Versuch einer Anweisung die Flöte traversiere zu spielen*. Berlin, 1752. Transl. Edward R. Reilly as *On Playing the Flute*. Second edition New York, 1985. *Essai d'une methode pour apprendre à jouer de la flute traversiere*. Berlin, 1752. R Paris: Zurfluh, 1975. (For excerpts, see *MacClintock*, 316–325 and *Strunk*, 577–598.)

Rameau, Jean-Philippe. *Traité de l'harmonie réduite à ses principes naturels*. Paris, 1722. R New York: Broude Brothers, 1965. Transl. Philip Gossett as *Treatise on Harmony*. New York: Dover, 1971.

Rousseau, Jean-Jacques. *Dictionnaire de musique*. Paris, 1768. Trans. William Waring as *A Complete Dictionary of Music*. London: J. Murray, 1779; R New York: AMS Press, 1975.

———. *Lettre sur la musique française*. Paris, 1753. Facs. in *La querelle des bouffons*, with introduction by Denise Launay, v. 1 (Geneva: Minkoff, 1973), 671–764. (For English translation, see *Strunk*, 636–654.)

Saint Lambert, Michel de. *Les principes du clavecin*. Paris, 1702. R Geneva: Minkoff, 1972. Transl. Rebecca Harris-Warrick as *Principles of the Harpsichord*. Cambridge: Cambridge University Press, 1984. Excerpt in *MacClintock*, 21–25.

Simpson, Christopher. *The Division Violist*. London, 1659. R New York: Schirmer, 1955.

Tartini, Giuseppe. *Lettera del defonto signor Giuseppe Tartini alla signora Maddalena Lombardini*. Trans. Dr. Burney as *A Letter from the late Signor Tartini to Signora Maddalena Lombardini*. London, 1779. R (in Italian and English) New York: Johnson Corporation, 1967.

Telemann, Georg Philipp. *Singe-, Spiel-, und Generalbass-Übungen*. Hamburg, 1733–1734. Ed. Max Seiffert. Berlin: Liepmannssohn, 1914. R Facs. Leipzig: Zentralantiquariat der DDR, Ausgabe für Bärenreiter Verlag, Kassel, 1983.

Tosi, Pier Francesco. *Opinioni de'cantori antici, e moderni.* Bologna, 1723. R Bologna: Forni, 1968. Transl. [John Ernst] Galliard as *Observations on the Florid Song.* Second ed., London, 1743. Ed. Michael Pilkington, London: Stainer and Bell, 1987. R New York: Broude Brothers, 1968. (See also the entry under Agricola.)

Viadana, Lodovico Grossi da. *Cento concerti ecclesiastici.* Venice, 1602. (The preface is in *Strunk,* 419–423; for excerpt, see *Rowen,* 150–153.)

Walther, Johann Gottfried. *Musicalisches Lexicon: oder, musikalische Bibliothek.* Leipzig, 1732. R Kassel: Bärenreiter Verlag, 1953.

Werckmeister, Andreas. *Die nothwendigsten Anmerkungen und Regeln wie der Bassus continuus oder General-Bass wohl könne tractiret werden.* Aschersleben, 1698. R Michaelstein: Kultur-und Forschungsstätte Michaelstein, 1985.

_____ . *Musikalische Temperatur.* 1691. Facs. ed. Rudolf Rasch. Utrecht: Diapason Press, 1983.

Appendix D:
Credits for Musical
Examples and Tables

Most of the musical examples were produced with *Theme* software (version 3.4) designed by Mark Lambert. Chapters 5 and 7 draw in a limited way upon two articles of mine: "Declamation and Expressive Singing in Recitative," in *Opera and Vivaldi*, ed. Michael Collins and Elise K. Kirk (Austin: University of Texas Press, 1984), 233–257; and "Performing Rameau's Cantatas," in *Early Music* 11 (October 1983), 480–489.

Sources for the musical examples and tables are listed below:

Example 2-1. G. F. Handel, *The Complete Sonatas for Violin and Basso Continuo*, ed. Terence Best (London: Faber Music Limited, 1983), 8.

Example 2-2. G. F. Handel, *The Complete Sonatas for Violin and Basso Continuo*, ed. Terence Best (London: Faber Music Limited, 1983), 12.

Example 3-1. Girolamo Fantini, *Modo per Imparare a sonare di tromba* (Frankfurt, 1638; R facs. ed. Nashville: The Brass Press, 1972), 67.

Example 3-2. Dario Castello, *Sonate concertate*, Book 1 (1621). Ed. Eleanor Selfridge-Field. Recent Researches in Music of the Baroque Era, v. 23. (Madison: A-R Editions, 1977), 39–40.

Example 3-3. Facs. from French ed. of *Quantz*, Table 24, 257–258.

Example 5-1. Francesco Geminiani, *A Treatise of Good Taste in the Art of Musick* (London, 1749), n. p.

Example 5-2. J.-H. d'Anglebert, *Principes de l'accompagnement* (1689). In J.-H. d'Anglebert, *Pièces de clavecin*, ed. Kenneth Gilbert (Paris: Heugel, 1975), 144.

Example 5-3. Thomas-Louis Bourgeois, *Psiché*, from *Cantates*, Book 2 (Paris, 1718).

Example 6-1a, b, c. Georg Muffat, *Florilegium secundum* (1698; R Baden-Baden: Koerner, 1990), 94–97.

Example 6-2a, b. Georg Muffat, *Florilegium secundum* (1698; R Baden-Baden: Koerner, 1990), 94–97.

Example 6-3a, b. Georg Muffat, *Florilegium secundum* (1968; R Baden-Baden: Koerner, 1990), 94–97.

Example 6-4. Biber, *Sonatae tam aris quam aulis servientes* (1676). *DTÖ*, v. 106–107, ed. Erich Schenk, 98.

Example 6-5. Marin Marais, *3ᵉ livre de pièces de violes* (Paris, 1711; R Basel: R. Ebner, 1978), 39.

Example 6-6. Michel Corrette, *L'école d'Orphée* (Paris, 1738). Facs. ed., (Geneva: Minkoff, 1972), 34.

Example 6-7. Hotteterre, *Principes de la flûte traversière, de la flûte à bec, et du hautbois* (1707). R Facs. of the Amsterdam, 1728 ed. (Kassel: Bärenreiter-Verlag, 1958), 21.

Example 6-8. Hotteterre's *Principes de la flûte traversière, de la flûte à bec, et du hautbois* (1707). R Facs. of the Amsterdam, 1728 ed. (Kassel: Bärenreiter-Verlag, 1958), 21.

Example 6-9. J. S. Bach, *NBA*, series 5/5: 4 and facs., p. viii.

Example 6-10. J. S. Bach, *BGA*, v. 36: 224.

Example 6-11. François Couperin, *L'art de toucher le clavecin* (Paris, 1717; R facs. New York: Broude Brothers, 1969, 29.

Example 7-1. Facs. from French ed. of *Quantz*, Table 23, fig. 5.

Example 7-2. Telemann, *Singe-, Spiel-, und Generalbass-Übungen.* (Hamburg, 1733–1734; R facs. Leipzig: Zentralantiquariat der DDR, Ausgabe für Bärenreiter Verlag, Kassel, 1983) n.p.

Example 7-3. Bérard, *L'art du chant* (Paris, 1755).

Example 7-4. (a) Rameau, *Pièces de clavessin* [sic] (Paris, 1724), (b) Rameau, *Les fêtes d'Hébé* (Paris, 1739), ed. Mary Cyr in *Rameau's opéra-ballet, Les fêtes d'Hébé*, unpublished Ph.D. disertation (University of California, Berkeley, 1975), 2: 369–370.

Example 7-5. Handel, *HandelW (Sonate da Camera)*. R (New Jersey: Gregg Press, Inc., 1965), 79: 15.

Example 8-1 a, b. Caccini, *Le nuove musiche* (Florence, 1601[1602]), facs. ed. (New York: Broude Brothers, 1973), n.p.

Example 8-2. Caccini, *Le nuove musiche* (Florence, 1601[1602]), facs. ed. (New York: Broude Brothers, 1973), n.p.

Example 8-3 a, b. Monteverdi, *MonteverdiW* 15/3:755 and 756, ed. Malipiero. Copyright by Universal Edition. Used by permission of European American Music Distributors Corporation, sole U.S. and Canadian agent for Universal Edition Vienna.

Example 8-4. Telemann, *Zwölf Methodische Sonaten*, ed. Max Seiffert (Kassel: Bärenreiter Verlag, 1955), 11.

Example 8-5. Mondonville, *Titon et l'Aurore*, act I, scene 3 (Paris, 1753); R facs. (New Jersey: Gregg International Publishers Limited, 1972), 70–71. Bérard, *L'art du chant* (Paris, 1755; R facs. New York, Broude Brothers, 1967), 32–33.

Example 8-6. J. S. Bach, *NBA*, series 5/7: 48.

Example 8-7. J. S. Bach, *BGA*, v. 42, p. 68–69; Vivaldi also in *BGA*, 42:294.

Table 8-1. Paris, Bibliothèque Nationale, Vm⁷1854. In D'Anglebert, *Pièces de clavecin* (1689), ed. Kenneth Gilbert (Paris: Heugel), p. x.

Table 8-2. François Couperin, *Pièces de clavecin*, book 1 (Paris, 1713), in *Complete Keyboard Works*, ed. Johannes Brahms and Friedrich Chrysander, series I: Ordres I-XIII, (London: Augener, 1888; R New York: Dover Publications, 1988), v. 1, xiv–xv.

Table 8-3. Bach, *NBA. Klavierbüchlein für Wilhelm Friedemann Bach*, ed. Wolfgang Plath (Kassel: Bärenreiter, 1962), series 5/5, p. 3.

Sources for the other tables are provided within the tables themselves. Credits for the figures are in the List of Figures at the front of the book.

Index

[**bold face** indicates the principal discussion for an entry]